MARGARET MEAD

MARGARET MEAD

A Biography
Mary Bowman-Kruhm

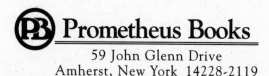
Prometheus Books

59 John Glenn Drive
Amherst, New York 14228-2119

Published 2011 by Prometheus Books

Inquiries should be addressed to
Prometheus Books
59 John Glenn Drive
Amherst, New York 14228–2119
VOICE: 716–691–0133
FAX: 716–691–0137
WWW.PROMETHEUSBOOKS.COM

15 14 13 12 11   5 4 3 2 1

Library of Congress Cataloging-in-Publication Data

Bowman-Kruhm, Mary.
    Margaret Mead : a biography / by Mary Bowman-Kruhm.
        p. cm.
    Originally published: Westport, CT. : Greenwood Press, 2003.
    Includes bibliographical references and index.
    ISBN 978–61614–391–6 (pbk.)
    1. Mead, Margaret, 1901–1978. 2. Women anthropologists—United States—
Biography. 3. Women anthropologists—Melanesia—Biography. 4. Ethnology—
Fieldwork—Melanesia. 5. Melanesia—Social life and customs. I. Title.

GN21.M36B85 2011
301.092—dc22
[B]   2011001707

Printed in the United States of America

Dedicated to Catherine Stover and Christine Paclawskyj, Johns Hopkins University, Montgomery Country Campus—talented and generous librarians who freely provided encouragement and much needed help obtaining books, articles, and tapes.

CONTENTS

ACKNOWLEDGMENTS

Special thanks for their thoughtful review of the manuscript to Dr. Amman Madan, Eklavya Institute of Educational Research & Innovative Action, Hoshangabad, India, and Dr. Richard Warms, professor of anthropology, Southwest Texas State University. Their support and the suggestions they offered enriched the book's content and were much appreciated. Thanks too to my husband, Carl Kruhm Jr., for his insights and observations when I was thinking through difficult sections, and to my editor, Wendi Schnaufer, whose substantive comments during this book's early stages provided direction that much enhanced the final product.

Thanks are also due to the Reverend Columba Gilliss, Dr. Hilary Lapsley, Kristen Mable (American Museum of Natural History), Dr. John McCreery, Dr. David Price, Dr. Dana Raphael, Dr. Rayna Rapp, Dr. Michael Salovesh, and Mary Wolfskill (Library of Congress) for prompt and helpful responses to my inquiries.

The author and publisher gratefully acknowledge permission for use of the following material:

Personal communication from Dana Raphael, Richard Warms and Michael Salovesh used by permission.

PREFACE TO THE PAPERBACK EDITION

To me, Margaret Mead is an American icon. Although those born after her 1978 death may not know specifics about her life, many recognize her name. For those who are older, her outreach from the 1930s to the 1970s was immense and people who were adults during those decades retain an image of her. When people discover I have written a book about Mead, some are quick to tell me they once saw her or heard her speak at their university. Others remember her as an engaging speaker on radio or a late night television program or they read her column in *Redbook* magazine; a few recall her as being prickly during an elevator ride or other encounter. A contributor to a knitting listserve on which I am a member adds, at the bottom of her posts, the quote attributed to Mead about the world's being changed only by a small group of committed citizens. A speaker from Oxford University in England used this same quote in a 2010 paper presented at a conference in Sweden on international relations. Margaret Mead touched and continues to touch many lives around the world and people respond to her name.

In the field of anthropology the controversy with Derek Freeman continues to be replayed. In fact, Robert A. LeVine began a May 2010 review of Paul Shankman's 2009 book, *The Trashing of Margaret Mead: Anatomy of an Anthropological Controversy*, with the question: "Can there ever be an end to the 27-year-old controversy over Margaret Mead's Samoan fieldwork of 1926?" (1108). My answer: No, not for many years.

In fact, Mead's work may now be referenced more than in the period immediately after her death. Virginia Yans (2009) noted a "recent revival of interest" (141) in Margaret Mead, Ruth Benedict, Reo Fortune, and Gregory Bateson. Since anthropologists would rather be in the field than the library, most have ignored investigating the extensive Mead collection—one of the largest private donations ever given the Library of Congress—which Yans describes as "almost thirty years of her collaborations with Ruth Benedict and a lifetime of personal and professional correspondence with many other social scientists" (141). I suspect anthropologists will give more attention in the future to what Yans writes is Mead's "unsurpassed collection of social science history" (142).

Yes, Mead should get attention from average folks fascinated in any way by the study of humankind and also by professionals in anthropology because she still has much to say to us today. Mead considered all the world part of anthropology and pontificated a great deal. While not always right, she was remarkably prescient. Among other current hot topics, she was concerned about US overdependence on fossil fuel, saw the United States as moving to become ever more a country of diversity, challenged education to instruct the whole child, and encouraged inclusion into the larger world by those with disabilities. Laurence A. Marschall (2009), in a review of a recent book about Mead, wrote, "The American Museum of Natural History, where she worked for most of her career, lists Mead among its fifty greatest treasures, and rightly so—she was as remarkable as any mammoth bone, gemstone, or feather cloak the museum has on display" (36).

For those still not convinced that Mead is an American icon: Few writers have their first book still in print over eighty years after it was initially published. Let's rejoice in having a celebrity with her values, integrity, drive, and intelligence. May we soon have another like Margaret Mead.

Mary Bowman-Kruhm

INTRODUCTION

Margaret Mead, anthropologist par excellence, traveled alone to Samoa, a South Pacific island, in 1925 when she was not yet twenty-four years old. Her nine months in Samoa and subsequent trips established Mead as an authority on the cultures of the South Pacific. Her books comparing those cultures to that of the United States became best-sellers and her provocative speeches and articles, which both angered and excited, made her name known across America. During her lifetime, Mead's likeness appeared on packets of sugar that pictured well-known Americans. She corresponded with presidents, was featured in cartoons, was a regular contributor to magazines, and was sought after as a guest on talk radio and television programs.

A few years before her death in 1978, someone leaving an auditorium after one of her speeches commented (Grinager, 1999: 75) that although her views were often difficult to accept, what she said was fifty years ahead of her time. In the twenty-first century, the world is just beginning to catch up with her ideas. Mead was always optimistic and opinionated, often irritating, seldom inarticulate, and never dull.

Nor was her personal life routine. For his 1988 edition of *Rethinking Psychological Anthropology*, a perspective of the dual fields of culture and personality, by Philip Bock, Presidential Professor Emeritus of Anthropology at the University of New Mexico, included pen-and-ink caricatures of noted anthropologists. The illustration of Mead, which was the only caricature of a woman and which depicted her with bared breasts, angered a number of readers. In the 1999 edition, Bock justified the cartoon by saying he felt Mead herself would have been amused because she liked to shock, and then he added, "If people are really outraged by [the] innocent drawing, they had best avoid actual knowledge of her life and ideas" (64).

This book explores Margaret Mead's life and ideas.

SIGNIFICANT EVENTS IN MARGARET MEAD'S LIFE

1901   Born December 16
1919   Entered DePauw University, Greencastle, Indiana
1920   Entered Barnard College, New York City
1923   Received BA from Barnard
        Began work on master's degree, Columbia University
        Married Luther Cressman
1924   Received MA in psychology from Columbia University
1925–1926   Conducted fieldwork in Samoa (nine months)
1926   Became assistant curator of ethnology at the American Museum of Natural History, New York City
1928   *Coming of Age in Samoa* published by William Morrow
        Divorced Luther Cressman
        Married Reo Fortune
1928–1929   Conducted fieldwork on Manus in Pere village, Admiralty Islands
1929   Received PhD in anthropology from Columbia University
1930   Conducted fieldwork on the Omaha Reservation, Nebraska (summer)
1931–1933   Conducted fieldwork in New Guinea
1935   Divorced Reo Fortune
1935   *Sex and Temperament in Three Primitive Societies* published by William Morrow
1936   Married Gregory Bateson
1936–1939   Conducted fieldwork in Bali and New Guinea
1939   Gave birth to daughter, Mary Catherine Bateson
1939–1945   Worked for US government (National Research Council, Committee on Food Habits, and other governmental organizations)

1950   Divorced Gregory Bateson

1953   Returned to Manus

1954   Became adjunct professor of anthropology at Columbia University

1960   Became president of the American Anthropological Association

1969   Became grandmother with birth of Sevanne Margaret Kassarjian

1972   *Blackberry Winter: My Earlier Years* published by William Morrow

1975   Became president of the American Association for the Advancement of Science
Elected to National Academy of Sciences

1978   Died in New York City, November 15
Awarded Presidential Medal of Freedom posthumously

Chapter 1

KITH AND KIN AS A GIRL IN PENNSYLVANIA (1901–1920)

> For children who have grown up with an ever-enlarging
> sense of their own autonomy and independence, intelli-
> gent handling of the opportunity for further education
> will come naturally and easily.
> —Mead and Métraux, *A Way of Seeing* (1961)

Seventeen-year-old Margaret Mead had spent the winter of 1918, during her final year of school before leaving her Pennsylvania home, studying the trigonometry and French she needed to attend the prestigious and expensive Wellesley College, outside of Boston, but her father had suddenly decided she should not attend college. Despite her father's advocacy of advanced education for women, he frequently risked money in precarious financial schemes and Margaret realized she was being unfairly punished for a business blunder he had made.

The family physician had come to their house, not to visit her father, but to talk to Margaret to convince her that money to attend college would be wasted. The more he talked, the less Margaret was swayed. Tension filled the room. Finally the doctor said, "Look at those useless little hands! Never did a day's work in their life and never will!" (Mead, 1972: 90).

Margaret felt rage rising in her. She was tired. Tired from cooking for her family of seven, tired from carrying a heavy course load at school, tired from sewing costumes for the school play, tired from her many other family responsibilities.

She exploded with fury when the doctor added, "You'd maybe make a good mistress, but a poor wife. You'd better study nursing!" (Mead, 1972: 90). Her parents had earned multiple college degrees and Margaret had anticipated attending college as well.

MEAD'S FATHER

Margaret Mead's father, Edward Sherwood Mead, sometimes called Sherwood by those close to him, earned a PhD in political economy in 1899 at the age of twenty-five. As a young man he quickly rose to full professor of economics at the Wharton School of the University of Pennsylvania, where he taught in the newly developing fields of finance and management.

Mead also directed the evening school program he helped establish in 1904, and several evenings a week traveled by train across Pennsylvania to lecture to part-time adult students. The range of his teaching stretched so far that he commented (Mead, 1972: 31) that he could walk into any bank on the East Coast and meet a onetime student. Building the evening school was a continuing challenge, but he believed strongly in the power of education. During his life he was ardently committed to helping the average person move ahead professionally by offering evening coursework.

Although Mead was a brilliant economist, he was also a risk-taker who frequently made bad personal investments and was short of money. Family finances bothered him little, since he believed, as a professor, that amassing great wealth would have been unseemly. He also thought that earning needed money was better than skimping and saving, a philosophy about handling money completely at odds with that of his wife, Emily.

Mead spent much time working on projects that dealt with the practical side of economics, like machinery to use the waste products from coal mining. His limited leisure time was spent reading Western magazines or investigating a current interest, like farming or gold mining. His wife would have preferred a staid husband who actively involved himself in the local community and who worked to further causes like women's suffrage, in which she fervently believed. Mead could also be sarcastic and demanding. His family interrupted their activities at his call and his secretaries carried out his excessive, caustic demands because they adored him.

In her autobiography, *Blackberry Winter: My Earlier Years*, Margaret Mead wrote that she prided herself on her ability to manipulate interactions with her father. When she was a young child, her father cautioned her against kicking wet leaves. He said that he would leave her and walk on alone if she persisted; when she continued to kick wet leaves, he did. Margaret sat down on the sidewalk and wailed about her "Bad Dada" (1972: 39) who had deserted his little girl until he returned in embarrassment to retrieve her amid stares from passersby.

Even when older, Margaret sought to control her own life rather than comply with her father's wishes. When she graduated from college in 1923, he offered her a round-the-world trip and a sizable supply of money on condition that she give up the idea of marrying. Margaret refused rather than acquiesce to his power, although she later realized that she married primarily because many young women in her generation were doing so.

Edward Mead was a practical person whose insights into how the world functioned were important to Margaret in her later fieldwork, and his advice on public speaking, honed over years of motivating tired students in evening classes, helped her renown as a speaker grow. Despite bumps in their personal interactions, Mead credited her father, since her mother's career was restricted by poor health and multiple children, for helping her discover her place in the world.

MEAD'S MOTHER

Emily Fogg grew up in Chicago and began her college studies at Wellesley College, but a reverse in family finances necessitated her returning home to the Midwest. She did office work and taught evening classes in Evanston, Illinois (Grinager: 44), until, with money saved and assistance from a fellowship, she enrolled at the University of Chicago, where she completed work for a bachelor's degree in 1896 and met her future husband. Family history claims that the first time Edward Mead saw this tiny, beautiful young woman sitting in the front row of a class, he decided she was the woman he would marry.

Emily continued limited work as a sociologist and pursued academic studies, eventually earning a master's degree and working toward a doctorate while rearing her family. Margaret believed that her mother's anthropological study was probably the first of its type in the

United States. Her mother's study, published in 1907 by the US Department of Agriculture, reported findings on Italian immigrants; Margaret built on this research for her own 1924 master's thesis. Emily was consumed with a desire to help causes, campaigns, and organizations in which she believed, especially women's rights. Indignant at the limitations put on women, she was ecstatic in 1920 when women at last gained the right to vote with passage of the Nineteenth Amendment to the Constitution.

Cooking and sewing were not on the list of skills at which Emily excelled; her interests were unique for a wife in the early 1900s. She walked miles because she felt it was good exercise, believed in breast-feeding babies, and painted the ceiling of her kitchen—activities generally unheard of for a refined woman of the time. She acted on her strong sense of responsibility for bettering society by spearheading projects like free public libraries and a job-training school for immigrant women, an outgrowth of her doctoral work.

Emily was far more concerned about causes than possessions. When her husband presented her with a bead necklace from Tiffany's, the elite jewelry store, she was horrified at such a waste of money on something so unneeded. The credit received when the necklace was returned to the store went unused for ten years, until Margaret purchased some spoons.

An ardent feminist, Emily believed in plainness, whether in food, girl's clothing, or household furnishings. The family's food was nutritious but not distinguished. Margaret yearned to wear frilly clothes, but Emily, like other progressive mothers who believed that long, loose trousers were sensible for active little girls, dressed her in bloomers. Money was given to the American Association of University Women rather than spent for a new rug. Similarly, Emily denounced political machines, women who did not use their minds and abilities, ostentatious wearing of furs and feathers, those who opposed the feminist cause, and injustice and prejudice, whether aimed at Jews, Catholics, blacks, immigrants, or other minority groups.

Although Margaret's mother had strong feelings and often upset dinners when she intensely expressed them, both fervor and fury were impersonally directed. Although she argued for the rights of those less fortunate, she tended to be cool and reserved around most people, was rather snobbish, and had little interest in ordinary people. To all individuals with whom she came in contact, however, she added charm and grace to her diminutive and attractive appearance. Just five feet tall, with long blond hair, she was a contrast to her husband, dark haired and six feet tall.

Despite her looks and demeanor, Emily had a naïveté and innocence that translated into a lack of sense of humor, and she did not exude warmth and playfulness. Margaret wrote in her autobiography that coordinating and hosting parties seemed a duty to her mother and that, by the age of eight, she took over party planning and preparations. Although Emily preferred purposeful meetings to social entertaining, she hosted "housecooling" parties when the family moved. Margaret said, "When I was a child, we moved twice a year. Having some kind of party was a perfect way to say good-bye to our many neighborhoods. My mother thought of it" (Grinager, 1999: 107). Emily Fogg Mead maintained a well-run, comfortable, unique household and in many ways provided a cultural milieu that fostered Margaret's lifetime love of learning.

MARGARET'S BIRTH AND THE TURN OF THE TWENTIETH CENTURY

Emily Mead's progressive ideas about social issues of the day extended into birthing, nursing, and rearing babies. Although Emily and Edward had not planned to start a family within the first year of their marriage, Emily immediately searched out sources to enhance her parenting skills and wanted to do "the best" (Mead, 1972: 18) she could for the baby. In an era in which most babies entered the world in their own homes, to Emily "best" meant birth in a hospital. On December 16, 1901, Margaret was the first baby born at the West Park Hospital in Philadelphia, a day reported to be bitterly cold, with the temperature staying below the freezing mark.

In 1901, Italian inventor Guglielmo Marconi received the first transatlantic radio transmission. Austrian scientist Karl Landstriner identified human blood groups A, B, and O. Lionel trains were the hottest toy and two of the best-selling books were Rudyard Kipling's *Kim* and Booker T. Washington's *Up from Slavery*. When President Teddy Roosevelt invited Washington to dine at the White House, many Southern whites, ardent supporters of racism who believed African Americans were genetically inferior to Caucasians, were furious.

The Civil War, however, had ended over a quarter century before and most citizens in the early 1900s were looking not to the past, but to the future. The United States of America stood on the threshold of being a world power. It now bridged the two great oceans and was bordered, as today, to the north by Canada and to the south by Mexico, but internal expansion from east to west would mean statehood for Oklahoma in 1907, followed by New Mexico and Arizona in 1912.[1]

Population growth in the continental United States from 1890 to 1900 increased by approximately 13 million people and so did inventions that promised a better life for the average citizen. With 1.5 million telephones in use in the United States, twenty-four years after their invention by Alexander Graham Bell, business and social contacts were suddenly easy to accomplish. King C. Gillette was on the cutting edge with an invention that provided men an alternative to shaving with a strap and straight-edge razor—a safety razor. And in their leisure time, people used their $1.00 Kodak Box Brownie cameras to take photographs.

The invention that captured the fancy of the public in the early years of the new century, however, was the automobile. The year before Mead's birth America's first auto show was held at Madison Square Garden in New York City, the city where Mead would spend much of her adult life. The cost of the most expensive car on exhibit was $4,000 (equivalent to $84,167 in 2001). Despite the beginning phase of a love affair with the automobile, cars would not become available to the masses until 1903, when Henry Ford received funding that enabled him to produce low-cost automobiles affordable to the average family.

Like the car, social change in the mainstream was slow. Great Britain's Queen Victoria died in 1901, and most people in the Western world were still mired in the manners and morals and Victorian lifestyle of the nineteenth century, a lifestyle characterized by a rigid code of behavior, conservatism, and pretension, especially among the middle and upper classes. Moral hypocrisy reigned; women in less affluent families were expected to work long hours for little pay at menial jobs, but women in middle- and upper-class families were placed on a pedestal that did not allow them to engage in thoughtful pursuits or meaningful careers.

The Mead household was not, however, like the average middle-class family at the century's turn. As well-educated social scientists, Mead's parents were deeply concerned with social issues. Mead embraced her parents' concerns throughout her life, but she credited her paternal grandmother with being "the most decisive influence in my life" (Mead, 1972: 45).

MARGARET'S GRANDMOTHERS

Martha Ramsay Meade (Margaret's parents dropped the final *e*) had been an elementary and secondary teacher and a school administrator in Ohio. After her husband, Giles F. Meade, a school superintendent, died in 1880, when she was only thirty-five years old, the principal of the school took over Giles Meade's position and Martha replaced the principal.

Sometime between Edward and Emily's 1900 marriage and Margaret's 1901 birth Martha announced to her son and daughter-in-law that she was moving to Pennsylvania to live with them. To Margaret, Martha Meade was known simply as Grandma. She provided Margaret with more affection than did her parents and was Margaret's teacher throughout most of her primary school years. She encouraged Margaret to record her observations and taught her how to cook, knit, and perform a variety of household tasks. Martha Meade's indifferent attitude toward social class influenced Margaret's egalitarianism. Although her mother's blatant support of feminism irritated Margaret, she relished her grandmother's stories about strong women.

Of Margaret's two grandmothers, Elizabeth Bogart Fogg, whose husband died when Margaret was two years old, had less influence on Margaret. She saw her maternal grandmother only for short visits but remembered her as an intelligent woman with a sharp tongue who could not relate to children. Elizabeth Fogg once complained that Margaret was tiresome, always writing plays no one wanted to hear. Margaret admired her grandmother's wit and vitality, although Elizabeth seemed more concerned with inconsequential appearance than substance. Born in 1849, she lived into her mid-nineties, after running away from a retirement home in which her children had placed her.

MARGARET'S SIBLINGS

In an era in which reliable birth control and safe abortion were not available, Emily Mead's rapidly growing family curbed her personal pursuits. After Margaret's birth in late 1901, Richard arrived in 1904, followed by three more daughters: Katherine in 1907, Elizabeth in 1909, and Priscilla in 1911.

Margaret felt that her father treated her with gender-equity and never felt lesser in her father's eyes because of her sex. Edward had affectionately applied the nickname "Punk" to Margaret when she was tiny, and after Richard's arrival he referred to him as "the boy-punk" and Margaret as "the original punk" (Mead, 1972: 19). Margaret later maintained that this terminology was an outward indication that her father considered females equal to males; otherwise he would have changed her name to "the girl-punk," with the implication that Richard had now gained in importance in the family.

Margaret had longed for a brother with whom to play pranks and roughhouse but Richard, often sick with a variety of illnesses, was not so sturdy a child as Margaret. Because their father was an extremely cautious man in matters concerning his children, Richard was restricted from many activities. Margaret and Richard were constant playmates, but in quiet pastimes. Often dressed alike, they ate most of their meals together and loved to sing together until time proved Richard to possess a fine, clear voice, unlike Margaret's.

One of the harshest assaults to family stability came with Katherine's death at nine months of age. Margaret had been allowed to name her, and everyone in the family, especially her father, cherished Katherine. When she died, the family slid into mourning and estrangement from each other.

Tensions ran high and even the birth of two daughters, Elizabeth and Priscilla, could not restore the early sense of harmony.

In *Blackberry Winter*, Mead remembered Elizabeth as "enthusiastic, loving, and devoted" (68). Elizabeth was also the creative one. She loved art and later taught it in the public schools of New York City and at Lesley College in Boston. Margaret hung Elizabeth's paintings wherever she lived to make her new quarters feel like home. One painting special to her was Elizabeth's first watercolor, of the New York Stock Exchange building, initially painted for their father.

Priscilla, the youngest and prettiest of the three Mead girls who survived infancy, disliked being told how beautiful she was. She was also smart, but not creative or studious according to Margaret. Priscilla didn't like school and didn't work as hard as Margaret did. Margaret also considered Priscilla self-centered and manipulative, although honest about orchestrating situations to get her way. Priscilla would later (Mead, 1972: 68) admit that she paid someone a compliment so he or she would comply with her wishes.

MULTIPLE HOUSES, PROGRESSIVE SCHOOLING

Since Edward's position necessitated travel, the family usually relocated with him. Seasonal household moves each year were common. During the University of Pennsylvania's academic year, the family rented from faculty members on sabbatical leave. These homes were close to the campus where Edward lectured during the day.

Like the winter homes, the summer homes were often new and strange to the children, with nooks to discover inside and, since the family preferred homes in small villages, with large backyards to explore outside. Margaret's leisure time as a child and later as an adult was spent in intellectual activities, like reading books, writing plays, and memorizing poetry (Mead, 1972: 74–75) rather than athletic activities, however.

Amid the many moves, the Meads usually returned to two homes. The first was a house with five acres of land in Hammonton, New Jersey, so that Emily could work on her doctorate by interviewing nearby Italian immigrant families. When Margaret was ten the family moved to Bucks County, Pennsylvania, a prestigious area outside Philadelphia. The family owned this farm until 1928, when Margaret was well on her way to becoming a renowned anthropologist. The frequent moves were instrumental in Margaret's later feeling that home "can be anywhere you make it" (Mead, 1972: 11).

Despite the frequent changes of residence, Margaret did not suffer multiple changes in schools. Many youngsters in the early 1900s stayed home from school to work on the family farm or care for smaller children, but they seldom opted out of the school system for educational reasons, as did the Mead children, who were home-schooled before the term was used or the concept developed.[2] Until she entered high school, Margaret was enrolled in school only for two years of kindergarten and half days during the fourth grade.

While frequent moves made homeschooling a likely choice, the type and quality of the instruction in local schools were also issues. Believing that children should be active participants in their own learning rather than passive receptacles, Emily arranged for hands-on instruction by a variety of local craftspeople, musicians, and artisans. Martha Meade concurred with Emily's educational philosophy and eagerly took on the job of home instruction in the academic areas during the children's elementary and middle-school years.

Her uncommon early education under her grandmother's tutelage encouraged Margaret to move in a variety of creative directions, especially in pursuits that included reading and writing. She devoured all sorts of books by time-honored authors like Sir Walter Scott, Jane Austen, and Charles Dickens and even series like the rags-to-riches stories of Horatio Alger, which her parents considered poorly written and a waste of time to read. Margaret also wrote her own stories and began writing poetry at the age of nine.

On May 14, 1911, when she was nine years old, Margaret began a diary in which even her earliest entries show the attention to detail that helped her future success as an anthropologist. She wrote, "I have decided to write a diary. . . . But I'm not going to just put down what happens in a crazy mater-of-fact [sic] way. . . . I'm going to just sort of tell a story, and say what I think about things, and people" (Library of Congress, d). Margaret then listed members of her family. She did not include her grandmother Martha but did mention household help. She also included a nurse, who had since left and whom she described as "saucy." Margaret reported that the nurse had told her grandmother "Shut up" to her face.

On May 14 she drew a detailed floor plan of her family's present home and noted that the previous day she and brother Richard had "had a fight" and that today she had got up early and learned to play the "Vick trola [*sic*]." Operating the Victrola, a spring-wound machine that played music by forcing a needle around grooves on a thin, twelve-inch disc, was probably a satisfying activity, equivalent to a child today learning to operate a family home entertainment system. After describing some pansies, Margaret concluded, "I've decided not to write a diary" and moved on to composing a story about a family named Emerson whose members were moving to a "summer place" (Library of Congress: d).

She did, however, return to making diary entries and in fact was a copious and methodical notetaker the rest of her life. Whether writing notes or more formal prose, she was never concerned about spelling. To Margaret, writing always seemed a process, with its result more important than strict adherence to the conventions of English writing.

At age eleven Margaret entered eighth grade at the Buckingham Friends School in Lahaska, Pennsylvania, about an hour's train trip from Philadelphia. The school had once been, and later was again, an excellent educational institution, but while Margaret was enrolled at Buckingham, lack of funding meant overcrowding and old textbooks, so her schoolwork was still supplemented with lessons from her grandmother Martha. At age fourteen Margaret entered Doylestown High School, where she repeated a year because of her young age. In the fall of 1918 she attended the Holmquist School in New Hope, Pennsylvania, a private school with a broad curriculum that included the languages she needed in preparation for college at Wellesley. Luckily, Margaret was a bright young girl who benefited from educational experiences that ranged from helping her grandmother make apple butter in a huge iron kettle and protecting shocks of wheat in a field from rain before it was threshed, to studying trigonometry and learning three years of French in one year.

PAINFUL INTRUSIONS IN HER CHILDHOOD

Margaret did not have a carefree, idyllic childhood. Her parents, educated and generally financially secure, seemed to genuinely care for each other, although real warmth was lacking. Nevertheless, some events in Margaret's life were painful and even life altering.

After Katherine's death, her father distanced himself from the other children. The death also caused a breach between her parents. Her father had several affairs with various women and considered a permanent relationship with one. When Martha stated she would remain with Emily and the children and Emily pointed out to her husband the cost of maintaining two households, he abandoned the other woman, turned his interests back to his family, and agreed to buy the Bucks County farm.

The family difficulties no doubt caused both emotional pain and additional work responsibilities for Margaret. Because Martha had always loved to comb Margaret's long brown hair and confide in her, Margaret was well aware of the anxieties of family members. Although insights into her parents' private lives were surely disconcerting to young Margaret, she developed an even closer bond with her grandmother through the confidences Martha shared.

As her mother's health worsened with successive pregnancies and emotional pressures, Margaret was needed to help care for the two youngest children and to assist with cooking and other household duties. Margaret, never athletic, had little time for carefree play. She also lost her sense of playfulness and later said that by the time she was ten years old, "I was a very sober little lady" (Grinager, 1999: 178).

The end to her father's philandering and the move to the Holicong farm in Bucks County, Pennsylvania, kept the family intact, but one can assume Edward's tendency toward ridicule and sarcasm and Emily's innate seriousness produced a gloomy atmosphere even when the family situation was stable.

At age eleven Margaret developed a close friendship with Miss Lucia, the daughter of the Episcopal church rector in Buckingham. Margaret recognized that Episcopalian rituals and beliefs would fill a void in her life. Her parents, definitely agnostic and leaning toward atheism, lacked any understanding of her desire and need for a relationship with God. Despite her father's sarcastic remarks, Margaret was baptized and became a lifelong Episcopalian. Very likely Miss Lucia's family represented the close, warm family Margaret did not have.

WRITING AS A LIFE PURSUIT

In *Blackberry Winter*, Mead wrote that her informal schooling had imbued her with a sense of American culture but had not provided formal academic instruction. She became very proficient, however, in reading and writing. During her high school years, Margaret wrote and produced theatrical events (like family dramatizations of a Shakespearean tragedy and high school plays), edited a high school magazine, wrote articles, began a novel, and learned the processes involved in the daily printing of a paper at the local newspaper office. She valued writing because her parents wrote, and it became a vital part of her life. Because few people were as skilled as she was, she realized that her ability with words made her special.

WORLD WAR I

Although the United States did not enter the Great War until 1917, it impacted the lives of people in the United States from 1914, when it began in Europe. In the early years of the war, the US public was strongly opposed to taking part and President Woodrow Wilson promised to keep the United States out of the conflict. As the war came menacingly closer, however, American sympathies were clearly allied with Great Britain, France, Belgium, Russia, Italy, and Japan in the fight against the imperialism of Germany, Austria-Hungary, Turkey, and Bulgaria, known as the Central Powers.

The war was soon extended beyond the borders of the countries initially involved. Attacks by German submarines (U-boats) on ships of countries that wanted to remain neutral, like Brazil, pressured those countries to enter the war or to break diplomatic relations with the Central Powers.

In the United States, papers were packed with stories of the war and reports claimed that U-boats had been sighted off America's East Coast. By 1917, after numerous acts of aggression by Germany, including sinking American merchant ships, the American people, including the Mead family, responded patriotically to the decision to declare war. Margaret made speeches to encourage support for World War I during her final year of high school. In one speech she referred to the consequences of the war, if Germany should win, as "too terrible to contemplate" (as cited in Howard, 1984: 34). She also created posters representing the threads that were ultimately woven into her entire life: internationalism, the status of woman, the value placed on childhood, vision for the future, and meaningful religion.

By the end of the war, about 5 million Americans volunteered or were drafted for the military; 116,000 soldiers eventually lost their lives. From all nations, an estimated 8.3 million soldiers were killed, 7 million soldiers were maimed for life, and 8 million civilians were killed. Movement of soldiers and ships precipitated the worst pandemic of disease in history, with at least 21 million people dying from the so-called Spanish influenza of 1918–1919.

The numbers of killed and wounded tell only part of the impact of the War to End All Wars. Ultimately, as an aftermath of the hostilities, World War I set the stage for a historic shift in the social and political composition of the world, when growth in communism resulted from extreme poverty among people most directly involved in the war.

ENGAGEMENT TO LUTHER CRESSMAN

Since Margaret had been schooled at home for so many years, Emily Mead was concerned about her daughter's social life during her high school years. She began to invite Margaret's school friends to their home the first Saturday evening of each month for dancing and refreshments and also often asked the teachers to join them at dinner. The Meads invited George Cressman, a teacher who was the school's commencement speaker, to dinner before the high school graduation ceremony and dance in the spring of 1917. Luther, one of George's five brothers, had just returned home from his junior year at Pennsylvania State College and was also invited.

Margaret and Luther danced that evening at the party and in her autobiography she remembered glowingly his wonderful skill at dancing, his delightful sense of humor, and his broad perspective of the world. In his autobiography, *A Golden Journey* (1988), written sixteen years after hers, Luther wrote that he barely recognized himself by Margaret's description of that evening and thanked her for it. Unfortunately, later that same night Margaret suffered an attack of appendicitis, and recuperation took several months. She did not see Luther again that summer, but he did send her his yearbook.

Luther, four years older than Margaret, returned to his final year of college in the fall, when Margaret began her senior year at Doylestown High School. She recalled seeing him once during the fall and then, during the Christmas holidays of 1917, they rapidly renewed their relationship at a family dinner at the Cressman home.

On December 31, 1917, bundled against the cold, with stars lighting the way and the only sound being their feet crunching in the snow, Margaret and Luther walked about a half mile. Cressman recalled that when they were nearly home, "wordless messages brought us to a stop and turned us facing each other. I embraced Margaret, and as she joined me, I said tenderly, 'I love you, Margaret'" (1988: 56). Margaret replied that she loved him, too, and they kissed. Given Margaret's age and Luther's future in a world entangled in World War I, personal plans had to be suspended and they told no one of their implied engagement.

Available sources, including his autobiography, represent Luther as a stable, studious, rational, and religious young man, one to whom Margaret probably looked to ease the feelings of discord in her own family. Unlike her father, he was sensitive, athletic, and witty without being sarcastic. In 1918, Luther graduated from Pennsylvania State College and was training for the military. Although World War I ended that year, Margaret, who had also just graduated from high school, was intent on matriculation, not matrimony. Marriage could wait; college couldn't.

FAMILY AGREEMENT ON COLLEGE

At age eighteen Margaret was at a turning point in her life. Like her mother and grandmother, she grew up expecting to be a professional woman, as well as a wife and mother. For her, future success depended on a college education.

The doctor's jab that she would "maybe make a good mistress, but a poor wife" and had "better study nursing!" infuriated her. To Margaret, his remarks were both unjust and illogical. The argument that she was not strong enough to study but strong enough to work as a nurse made no sense. She felt justified in her desire to attend college.

Eventually, Margaret's mother swayed her father. His alma mater, DePauw University in Indiana, seemed a workable compromise. Reason prevailed, especially since Mead's professorial father held education in high esteem, a view frequently clouded by his bad business investments and controlling personality. Her father's philosophy toward education, her mother's and grandmother's support, and her own determination to attend college primed her for attending DePauw University in the fall of 1919. Margaret Mead did not realize what an unhappy year she would have.

Chapter 2

FROM INDIANA TO OCEANIA
(1920–1925)

The smallest journey may be forever.
—Mead, *Blackberry Winter* (1972)

Margaret Mead's introduction to campus life in the fall, 1919, was the beginning of an awful year at DePauw University. The daughter of an aunt's friend had written to her over the summer, enthusiastically inviting her to attend a rush party hosted by Kappa sorority soon after she arrived on campus as a freshman. Because Margaret realized being selected for membership as a Kappa depended on her impressing the sorority girls hosting the event, she had worn a dress she herself had designed, sewn by a dressmaker her mother enlisted to translate Margaret's wishes into a college wardrobe. Although the design was meant to symbolize huge poppies in a field of wheat, Margaret soon realized that the dress, very different from those worn by the other young women, was to midwestern eyes unfashionable. The friend's daughter ignored her and, when the bids to join were distributed, the sorority had excluded Margaret from membership.

In *Blackberry Winter*, Mead recalled that the entire evening was confusing to her, since she did not realize the sorority members had received a signal that she would not be an appropriate member. The passage of time did not diminish her indignation. In the early 1940s, when Mead was asked to speak to the Panhellenic Association, a consortium of sorority representatives, on the topic of democracy, she made it clear she saw the sorority system as destructive to young women's sense of self. Mead did, however, accept the 1940 National Achievement Award from Chi Omega sorority, which in 1930 had been the first national women's organization to present an award for the outstanding achievement of a woman.

OTHER PROBLEMS AT DePAUW

The rest of Margaret's wardrobe was also unlike anything worn by stylish young women in central Indiana and Margaret was perceived as different in other ways. She had taken with her a tea set, books, and pictures as dormitory room decorations, but these, along with the color scheme she selected, were to the eyes of her midwestern classmates unusual. And she didn't chew gum.

As the weeks went by, Margaret was excluded from activities and was made to appear foolish by the other students. Classmates poked fun at her accent by encouraging her, especially in front of their visiting relatives, to pronounce words like *been*, which she pronounced as "bean" rather than the native "bin." Margaret probably unwittingly encouraged harassment with manners that her classmates considered snobbish, like dressing for dinner even when eating informally.

Mead never minded being thought of as different if the difference was based on her competence. In fact, while growing up, she had thrived on hearing her family constantly remark that there was no one quite like Margaret. Hearing her uniqueness touted with pride within her family was quite acceptable, but sensing strangers imply it with derision was painful, especially because she believed her classmates' comments were motivated by frivolous, superficial reasons.

Mead also realized that her goals were not those of the typical DePauw student. She felt her classmates came for the pleasures of campus life—fraternities and sororities and football games. Her feelings about her experiences at DePauw were still evident over half a century later when she tartly noted in *Blackberry Winter* that the male students hoped to become "good Rotarians in later life and their wives good members of the garden club" (1972: 97).

Several other students on campus who were similarly excluded from the mainstream of campus life banded together. One of these, Katharine Rothenberger, became a lifelong friend of Mead's. Because the area around DePauw was firmly Methodist, religion seems to have been an underlying cause for their ostracism. Mead was Episcopalian, Katharine was the daughter of a Lutheran minister, and other friends were Catholic, Greek Orthodox, and Jewish.

When Margaret tried to join the local Young Women's Christian

Association (YWCA), she suffered an added insult. Only members of Evangelical religions were eligible and as an Episcopalian she was excluded from joining. These acts of discrimination against her, she later wrote, seemed mild in comparison to injustices carried out against various minority groups, but nevertheless her entire year in the Midwest was a distasteful experience. Her DePauw experience showed Margaret how cruel people could be and she learned achievement would come only from her own hard work and not through membership in a group perceived as having status.

Margaret threw her efforts and energies into activities in which she could excel. She wrote a stunt that was performed by the freshman dormitory in a competition among dormitories and sororities. She worked to be selected for the English honors society, whose name, ironically enough, was Tusitala, the name given author Robert Louis Stevenson when he journeyed to Samoa in the late nineteenth century. Little did she realize what an important role Samoa would play in her life.

Two other accomplishments won Margaret campuswide recognition. Both of these involved her tall, red-haired friend Katharine Rothenberger. First, Mead wrote both words and music for a May Day pageant that involved all of the university's female students and cast Katharine and herself in starring roles. As king and queen of the May, both wore lavish lavender costumes. Katharine's suit featured a velvet ruff around her neck, Margaret's a long, full skirt with regal tiara. Margaret also designed the May Day freshman float.

Second, as campaign manager in Katharine's successful bid to become the first female student government vice president, Margaret was resourceful and not above a little chicanery in setting the sorority candidates against each other and enabling an outsider to win election. Her adroitness in managing Katharine's campaign encouraged her to flirt briefly with the idea of a political career.

These victories in her fight to overcome initial rejection were comforting, but Mead always considered her academic experiences at DePauw more rewarding than social ones. She had an excellent English professor, Ralph Pence, who she later said gave her unequaled instruction in writing, instruction she obviously found useful in later developing a style that served her well.

Despite Pence's mentoring and with regrets only about leaving her friend Katharine, Margaret happily said goodbye to DePauw at the end of her freshman year. Mead's experience had convinced her that having males and females together in an educational setting was detrimental to young women. This conclusion, along with missing the intellectual milieu the East Coast offered, contributed to her decision to attend a women's college. And, Luther was in New York.

LUTHER'S ROLE IN MARGARET'S LIFE

At Margaret's suggestion, Luther, whose family was Lutheran, joined the Episcopal Church. Since coercion would be entirely in character for Margaret, one might assume that she pressured him to convert, but Luther wrote in his memoirs only that Margaret suggested the idea and that she was correct in assuming he would feel comfortable with Episcopalian ritual and liturgy. (Cressman: 57)

Luther taught German and Latin at a private boys school for several months after he was discharged from the army and then, in the fall of 1919, when Margaret entered DePauw University, he entered General Theological Seminary in New York City to study for the Episcopal priesthood. He was beginning his second year of study when Margaret arrived in New York to enroll in Barnard College, the women's counterpart to Columbia University.

If Margaret wanted to be closer to Luther, Barnard was a logical choice; however, although Margaret noted briefly in *Blackberry Winter* that she and Luther saw each other during her years in college, he seemed very much a shadowy figure, more an accessory than an integral part of her life. Margaret's mind was focused on a successful college experience.

From 1920, when she left DePauw University, through her entire life, Mead's career was characterized by a litany of seemingly small decisions that sparked life-shaping events, referred to by social psychologist John C. Glidewell as life's "choice points" (1970: 2). One of these choice points was her decision to continue her college education at Barnard College in New York City.

NEW YORK CITY AND LIFELONG FRIENDSHIPS

Mead arrived in New York City in the fall of 1920 for her sophomore year. World War I had ended, the country was alive again, and no city was more bustling. There a newcomer could find a variety of opportunities and excitement, as did Mead in 1920 and for the rest of her life. Despite numerous trips later around the world, she considered herself a city person, and New York was the city to which she always returned. *Margaret Mead: Some Personal Views*, a collection of questions frequently asked Margaret and her responses, was published shortly after her death, and included the question, "In what place in the world would you like most to live?" Mead's response was, "Where I do live—in New York City" (1979: 253).

When she arrived at Barnard College, Mead was searching for more than a college education. She also wanted friends who would give her the "intellectual feast" (Mead, 1972: 97) she had longed for at DePauw. Ultimately she hoped to find a career that would provide her not only with work, but also with a cause, a crusade into which she could throw her energies. At Barnard, she found everything she was seeking.

Margaret's group of friends at Barnard went by several disparaging names that they adopted with a kind of mischievous glee. During her first year, the head of the dormitory apartments called them "a mental and moral muss" (Mead, 1972: 110) and they lighted on it. The name that stuck, however, was bestowed by a favorite professor of drama, Miss Minor Latham, who said in a thick Southern drawl that the young women sat up all night reading poetry and came to class looking like "Ash Can Cats."

In her first year at Barnard, Margaret and Léonie Adams, her friend and sometime roommate, were principal members of the Cats; others included Pelham Kortheuer, Deborah Kaplan, and Mary Anne McCall, known as "Bunny." Although members more or less entered and exited according to circumstances, the group considered themselves a "family" and developed a chain of kin, with members assuming the roles of "parents" and "children." Eventually, "grandchildren" and, by Margaret's senior year, a "great-grandchild" was added to the group.

Because of limited dormitory space at Barnard, the Ash Can Cats lived in three different apartments during Mead's college years. As with many city colleges, numerous students lived at home and commuted to classes; several of these commuters often camped out in the Cats' apartment and became group members. The composition of the Cats was fluid until several years after Mead's graduation, when a core group solidified, continued to see each other, and maintained lifelong friendships. Marie Eichelberger, older than most of the Cats because she contracted tuberculosis in high school and spent several years recovering before entering Barnard, merits mention as an especially important friend because of her future multiple roles as confidant, friend, and tireless helper in numerous areas of Mead's life.

Many socially conservative older people felt disillusioned with the shift in America's post–World War I moral and social values and were opposed to young women who rebelled against the established Victorian lifestyle. Although most of Margaret's friends at Barnard weren't flappers who threw away their inhibitions and conventions of conduct, they enjoyed freedom from earlier societal constraints on unmarried women. Among unmarried women of the 1920s bare arms and necks were in, hair was bobbed, skirts were short, legs could show, cosmetics were okay, cigarettes were chic, hopes were high, and the world belonged to them.

The Cats took advantage of a world newly opened to unmarried females. They were bright, brainy, talented young women who were curious about the world and were not afraid to show their intelligence. They took part in mass meetings on social issues, such as the trial of Nicola Sacco and Bartolomeo Vanzetti, Italian immigrants executed despite the belief of many people that they did not receive a fair trial in a 1920 murder case because of their anarchist political views.

The Cats stuffed envelopes and even picketed for causes they believed in. When Mead told her mother that she and her friends had joined a picket line, risked arrest, and were pelted with empty spools thrown from factory windows, her mother applauded—until Margaret reported that they yelled, "Ain't you got no conscience, dearies?" (1972: 59) at scabs who crossed picket lines. Emily was horrified that Margaret would say "ain't" in support of any cause. The Cats hosted impromptu debates in their apartment on a regular basis. They and their friends argued with each other informally late into the night about both significant social issues and inconsequential topics of interest. Margaret loved such open discussions, although she often opted to retire early. One friend and Ash Can Cat "grandchild," Louise Rosenblatt, characterized her long friendship with Mead as a running debate that lasted until Mead's death.

The Ash Can Cats also enjoyed both reading and writing poetry. The Cats especially relished the lyrics of poet and writer of short plays Edna St. Vincent Millay. On the first day of May 1925, several of them waited outside Millay's Greenwich Village house to gift her with a traditional May Day basket of flowers. They were thrilled when the famous writer acknowledged them and recognized the name of the shy but delighted Léonie Adams as a published poet.

PHYSICAL PROBLEMS AND CAREER CONSIDERATIONS

Toward the end of her first year at Barnard, Mead began experiencing pain and loss of control in her right arm. The diagnoses was neuritis, a rather vague designation of an ailment that forced her to wear her arm in a sling and take examinations orally. Mead's father, again short of cash, initially responded by threatening to cut her college career short, which he later decided against. Mead continued to have assorted pains in her arms and legs throughout her life.

By the time Mead was a senior, she had discounted a career as a writer. Ambitious and aspiring to be the best in her chosen field, Mead realized she would never be so good a writer as Léonie Adams. Margaret entered her senior year with a joint major in English and psychology. She took a course on the psychological aspects of culture, taught by William Fielding Ogburn, whose 1923 book on social change indicated his special field of expertise, and also elected to take a course in anthropology rather than philosophy.

While psychology primarily focused on individuals, anthropology focused on groups of people and the traits they held in common. Most social scientists, overtly or covertly, assumed that Western cultures were superior because the people who belonged to them were held to be biologically superior. As the nineteenth century turned into the twentieth, many American anthropologists, led by Franz Boas, were developing ways of observing and recording culture that recognized each society's strengths. Gone was the notion of ranking both cultures and human biology on a hierarchical scale.

Like many students, Mead was allured by the possibilities the new field of anthropology offered, although the entire full-time anthropology department at Columbia and Barnard was composed of only one man, Franz Boas. He was the catalyst for Mead's finding, in anthropology, an outlet for her energies and intelligence.

FRANZ BOAS AND CULTURAL RELATIVISM

Franz Boas was born in Minden, Germany, in 1858, into a liberal Jewish family. He was a short, well-proportioned man, handsome when viewed from his right side. A horrible scar ran down the left side of his face and his left cheek drooped, allegedly inflicted in a duel between Boas and someone who had made an anti-Semitic remark toward him when he was a student. Boas received his doctorate in physics from the University of Kiel in Germany but then changed disciplines, first to mathematics, then to physical geography, then to cultural geography, and ultimately to anthropology, to which Boas devoted his life. Although his interests changed, his demanding and rigorous scholarship and high standards for academic excellence for himself and those with whom he worked did not.

In 1883–1884, Boas traveled to the Arctic to study the Eskimo. Prior to this trip he was convinced that natural environment explained cultural differences. He soon realized, however, that the problem was more complex and that the people themselves were responsible for many elements of a culture. Some of these were rational; others were illogical but still important to understanding that culture. Boas continued on to Newfoundland and New York City before returning to Germany. He made valuable contacts on this North American trip and on a subsequent trip the next year when he investigated Native American culture in British Columbia.

In 1888, Boas emigrated from Germany to accept an entry-level position at Clark University in Worcester, Massachusetts. Clark was then a poorly endowed school with seemingly little to offer compared to his positions at the Royal Ethnographic Museum and the University of Berlin, located in an exciting, cosmopolitan city of culture. He later said his visits to the United States had convinced him he belonged among the rugged individualists in a new, expanding nation. An additional factor in his decision was the probability that growing anti-Semitism would restrict his scientific pursuits, as Germany became increasingly conservative under Chancellor Otto von Bismarck.

By age forty-three, Boas was curator at the American Museum of Natural History and professor of anthropology at Columbia University. But after a few years he left the museum to teach full-time at Columbia, including undergraduate courses at Barnard, and remained there until he retired in 1936. At the time of his death in 1942, Boas was rightly referred to as the founder of modern American anthropology.

Boas had a great deal of integrity and was a brilliant intellectual who did not hesitate to let his position be known on topics about which he felt strongly, even at the risk of personal grief. In 1919 Boas publicly criticized four unnamed anthropologists for espionage under the pretense of fieldwork during World War I. Rather than confront the ethical question he raised, Boas was censured by the American Anthropological Association (AAA), an action that removed him from the AAA's governing council (Price 2000).[1]

As a professor, Boas was demanding. For those eager to learn, he delivered, without use of notes, lectures that encouraged thought rather than fed information. During his entire adult life, Boas dedicated his considerable energy and vision to changing the face of anthropology. His students who became well known include, in addition to Mead and Luther Cressman, noted anthropologists Ruth Benedict, Melville Herskovits, and Alfred L. Kroeber, who helped Benedict on her first fieldwork, and fiction writer and folklorist Zora Neale Hurston, whose novel *Their Eyes Were Watching God* is considered a classic of African American literature.

Boas's personal background and scholarly work convinced him that cultural relativism was both an accurate and a morally correct concept with which to explain differences among peoples. At the time, the predominant view among scientists was that all cultures progressively moved from savage to civilized. To Boas, that was a biased, white, Western view of a society's evolution. He believed that differences among cultures were the result of different cultural histories and a culture's values and norms resulted from that culture's unique history. Any trait common in a culture should be viewed in relation to that culture only; a trait that makes sense in one culture may seem curious in another. Cultural relativism, with its focus on accepting and respecting the shared attitudes, values, morals, goals, and patterns of behavior of a culture, was an extension of this perception. Cultural relativism implies that no culture is superior to another, as opposed to ethnocentrism, which views some groups (usually Western cultures) as superior.

As a leading proponent of cultural relativism, Boas was especially committed to exploring rapidly changing cultures that had been previously isolated and capturing information before it was forever lost. For him, this commitment seemed more a campaign than a job, and he passed this sense of urgency on to his students. To carry out his determined efforts to study these fading cultures, he recruited women to enter the graduate anthropology program at Columbia, served as their mentor, and nourished their work. He remained, however, a man of his times and his own culture, as he expected women who toiled for him to work for less pay than men and he usually recommended the latter for job advancement.

RUTH BENEDICT

Ruth Fulton Benedict gained inspiration and a love of anthropology from Boas and was one of those toiling for him as a teaching assistant when Mead met her. Although the Ash Can Cats and numerous friends like Marie Eichelberger played early and lasting roles in Mead's life, her closest and most enduring female friendship was with Benedict.

Ruth was born in New York City but grew up on the farm of her maternal grandfather near Norwich, in midstate New York. Her father died before she was two years old and, probably in part because her mother's compulsive grieving traumatized young Ruth, she became a very private person, given to self-doubt and depression. An excellent student, she attended Vassar through the generosity of a benefactor and spent several unhappy years in social work and teaching. In 1914 she married Stanley Benedict, a biochemistry professor at Cornell University Medical School in New York City, and the couple seemed to have been happy at first. When Ruth was unable to have children, she felt stuck in a marriage that was less than exciting and not even satisfying; they finally separated in 1930. Ruth was thirty-three years old when she became a doctoral student in anthropology at Columbia in 1921, the year before she met Mead.

Benedict received her doctorate in 1922 and continued to work at Columbia, for which she was paid from teaching assistantships or funding primarily obtained by the resourceful Boas, neither source either lucrative or permanent. In a position similar to administrative assistant, she was an essential communications link between Boas and his students in the field and "she probably knew more about what was going on in American anthropology in the 1920s than any other single person, including Boas" (R. Warms, personal communication, January 23, 2002).

Because of partial deafness, fieldwork and teaching were difficult. She had trouble learning languages and others had to interpret for her while in the field. Classroom discussions were initially an ordeal, later simply a chore because she battled so hard to succeed. Her lectures were delivered in a low, halting voice, but she knew her content and she often grabbed students' attention with her powerful insights into anthropology.

The students, including Mead, saw Benedict as distant, middle-aged, and dowdy, with drab brown hair that the hairpins of the day were unable to hold in place. Although she felt that Benedict's beauty grew with age and confidence, Mead wrote that when she met Ruth, her beauty "was completely in eclipse" (1974a: 3).

Benedict first observed Mead riding home on the subway after attending a lecture with a group of friends. They later became acquainted when Ruth assisted Boas in the elective anthropology class in which Mead had enrolled, sometimes traveled together to view exhibits at the American Museum of Natural History, and met informally for lunch.

Mead credited her career choice to Benedict. At lunch one day in March 1923, Ruth told Margaret that she and Professor Boas had nothing to offer Mead "but an opportunity to do work that matters" (Mead 1972: 123). If Ruth's comment sounds dramatic and poignant, it was literally quite true. Job opportunities for female anthropologists were limited to a few teaching positions, primarily at women's colleges. Nevertheless, Margaret was intrigued by the chance to capture elements of cultures fast being marginalized and could not resist Benedict's challenge. In a March 11, 1923, letter to her grandmother, she wrote, "I would so like to be an Anthropologist." But, she added, it was "non-lucrative" (Library of Congress: a).

Ruth and Margaret enjoyed sharing poetry, including their own, as well as discussing anthropology, but the suicide of Marie Bloomfield, with whom Mead was acquainted but not close, deepened their bond. When Mead realized Marie was alone after being discharged from the hospital following a long bout with measles, Mead settled her into her dormitory room and promised to return. Then, when a friend's hysteria after an exam caused temporary blindness, Mead cared for her over the weekend and, in the interim, Marie killed herself from a dose of cyanide. Pressure from the college administration to explain matters to the newspapers by saying that Marie was insane added to Mead's personal guilt. Benedict's immediate response was a sensitive note followed by long talks that helped Margaret move past the horror of the situation and added to the personal trust they were developing in each other.

MARRIAGE

Margaret received her bachelor's degree in psychology from Barnard in the spring of 1923 and Luther was ordained a priest that same spring. Although her father offered her a trip around the world and a generous monetary allowance on condition that she didn't marry, she and Luther decided, after being engaged almost six years, that they could support themselves and pay for their college expenses as a married couple. Luther was well on his way to a doctorate in sociology at Columbia University. Margaret was committed to working on a master's degree in psychology the next year, although she was now enthusiastic about a career in anthropology and would begin working concurrently on a doctorate with Boas while completing her master's thesis. She also had a part-time position as secretary to Professor William Fielding Ogburn, a brilliant sociologist known for his rigorous research standards. Both Margaret and Luther studied with him and Margaret credited Ogburn with finding enough money to keep their personal finances afloat. Ogburn became a lifelong friend and was especially close to Luther.

In September 1923, Luther and Margaret exchanged vows at Trinity Episcopal Church, the small church where she had been confirmed, in Buckingham, Pennsylvania. A reception luncheon was held at the Meads' nearby home. Although Luther wrote that he and Margaret had no reservations about marriage, no record exists of Margaret's ever writing or saying that Luther was the love of her life. A passion to marry may have induced her to reject her father's offer, but she does not seem to have felt passionately about Luther. He did, however, seem a prudent choice for an ambitious professional woman eager to marry.

THE PLIGHT OF THE MARRIED WOMAN

Unmarried women had more freedoms in the 1920s than in previous generations, but society was not nearly so supportive of women once they married. In some jobs, like that of a telephone operator, a woman needed her husband's permission to work. Minimum-wage laws applied only to men. Even in the professional fields, management assumed a working wife would and should be supported by a husband and so paid her less or fired her; for example, the law in almost all states required a woman who married to forfeit a teaching position. While a single woman could gain satisfaction from working, a married woman was expected to serve as a satellite to her spouse and settle down to her "real" vocation of wife and mother.

Although Mead decried her mother's feminism, she was too ambitious and too independent to accept a supportive role in a marriage. Margaret's choice of Luther seems to have been based less on fiery passion and more on desire to have a fiancé and later a husband who offered Margaret security and allowed her to pursue her chosen agenda. While other young women spent time being tied up with boyfriend problems and tied down with relationships, Mead was attached but not confined.

Mead recognized that Luther was in the minority among men of the 1920s. He would willingly share household responsibilities with a professional wife and embrace the roles of supportive spouse and steadfast father. While her family probably was not surprised, the first indication to the outside world of an equal partnership with Luther came with the decision to retain her maiden name.

Mead wrote a chatty letter to her grandmother on December 7, 1923, several months after her marriage. The top of the letterhead featured the name "Margaret Mead" in block print. In the letter, Mead primarily discussed holiday plans and gifts. She added a postscript vertically down the right side of the page noting that Luther's parents "weren't a bit shocked at my keeping my own name," and that Luther's mother was "perfectly willing to call me Margaret Mead" (Library of Congress: e).

In *Blackberry Winter*, Mead wrote that she was influenced to keep her maiden name by her mother's belief that women should keep their own identity. Mead made the right decision on this seemingly minor point. In later life, as her popularity (and the number of ex-spouses) grew, a simple, alliterative, easy-to-remember name certainly benefited her and increased her recognition in distant parts of the world.

The couple pooled their money, but it was quickly consumed with living expenses and college tuition for both of them. Although Margaret wrote in *Blackberry Winter* that they supported themselves on income from her part-time job and a small fellowship of her husband's, Luther corrected the record in his memoirs. He had turned down a fellowship because to accept it would have meant giving up an extremely gratifying part-time position at a small Episcopal mission church in Brooklyn. Regardless of the source, money was limited and they entertained with meals of ground beef served in a multitude of ways.

Both Margaret and Luther recalled their first two years of marriage as peaceful, with neither of them fighting, quarreling, or even being disagreeable, although miscommunication and inevitable tensions were sometimes present. In reflecting on the early years of their marriage, Luther wrote that as soon as they returned from their honeymoon, they became aware of tensions caused by a stressful academic schedule that allowed little time for each other. "That Margaret had chosen academic performance was a storm flag of warning we both recognized for the voyage ahead" (Cressman 1988: 126).

They also realized that high academic performance as an anthropologist required Margaret to work in the field with separation for extended periods. Luther later commented that they did not relish such separation but accepted it as part of their chosen lifestyle.

FIRST FIELDWORK IN SAMOA

In *Anthropologists and What They Do*, first published in 1959, Mead wrote that organizing fieldwork requires two decisions: the first involves location and a culture to study and the second involves a problem on which to focus. The order in which these are selected isn't relevant. An anthropologist may first pick people and location and then ask himself or herself what problem could be investigated or, alternatively, start with a problem and then choose the location and people that would best answer the problem.

For Mead's first foray into the field, final approval of both location/culture and problem rested with Boas. Resolving the issue of location required especial negotiation between Mead and Boas. Attending the British Association for the Advancement of Science in Toronto, Canada, in 1924 convinced Mead she should conduct fieldwork with her own group of "people," a culture with whom she would be associated her entire career. According to Luther, finding her own people "became a driving force" (Cressman 1988: 112).

On the other hand, Boas, the preeminent leader in anthropology, was not about to allow the limited number of anthropologists in the field to carry out research of their choice haphazardly. In addition, although Boas wanted to place anthropologists among those cultures fast disappearing with the encroachment of Western civilization, with the goal of gaining extensive, coordinated information, he had a strong sense of responsibility that his students, many of whom were female, should work in areas where they would be relatively safe from danger.

Boas failed to convince Mead to work in the Southwest with Native Americans. The Southwest was too safe in a number of ways. While Margaret knew she would probably be physically safe, she also knew her chances for adventure were slim, as she would be one among many anthropologists already active there.

For her first fieldwork, Margaret would not accept a location and a people whom she did not want to study. Luther wrote that in Mead, Boas had a "pressing problem" (Cressman 1988: 492). Boas recognized that Margaret was intelligent, headstrong, and ambitious and he wanted to provide the same support he would provide for a male eager to embark on his first fieldwork outside the United States. Polynesia became Mead's location of choice, and Boas capitulated, provided she go to American Samoa, where US ships regularly docked and whose government was then administered by the US Navy.

More easily resolved was the choice of problem she would investigate. Victor Barnouw, professor of anthropology and department chairperson at the University of Wisconsin-Milwaukee, credited Mead in his book *Culture and Personality*, with introducing the practice of fieldwork centered around a problem. Traditionally, anthropologists had attempted to record information about multiple elements within a culture, with the assumption that these so-called primitive cultures were quickly disappearing and every shard of information was pertinent. Barnouw noted that, although some of Mead's ethnographic reports were in this tradition, her best-known works targeted a specific problem, relevant both to the culture being studied and the culture of the United States. "Boas himself," wrote Barnouw, "deserves some credit for this deviation from his own approach, for he helped to suggest and to discuss Mead's research problems with her before she went to Samoa on her first field trip" (1979: 89).

Mead initially preferred her choice of problem to involve cultural change, but when Boas suggested she study adolescence, she agreed to investigate the difficulties young girls encounter in passing through adolescence. If Samoan females passed easily from girl to young adult, then the storm and stress prevalent during adolescence in Western civilizations could be seen as caused by culture. If Samoan females also had difficulties, adolescence could be viewed as a natural part of life—a function of biology, not culture. The work of Boas and his students overwhelmingly supported the importance of culture over biology. Freudian psychology viewed adolescence as a time of turmoil that was biologically based, while Boas believed this turmoil to be culturally based.

Boas supported Mead's efforts to obtain funding from the Board of Fellowships in the Biological Sciences of the National Research Council, and on April 30, 1925, Mead received news that her fellowship had been approved. With an offer from her father to pay for her transportation to Samoa, a gift she had in fact manipulated to secure, her fieldwork plans were finalized. Characteristically, she celebrated the next day—May Day—with the Ash Can Cats. This was the exciting May Day when Edna St. Vincent Millay acknowledged their gift of a basket of flowers.

WHY SAMOA?

Why did Mead travel halfway around the world to Samoa? Why investigate the angst of Samoan girls' adolescent years? Decisions made during negotiations with Boas were based on sound reasoning and logical rationale.

First, she had already researched aspects of life on Polynesia and had presented a paper on Polynesian tattooing in Toronto at a 1924 conference. She was intrigued with the faraway and seemingly exotic isles of Oceania. Besides, a joke among anthropologists at the time was that Native American families in the Southwest were made up of five people: a father, a mother, two children, and an anthropologist. Mead was not about to compete in that arena. The relatively unfamiliar people of Polynesia were to be her "people."

Second, Mead was an ambitious, competent female trying to succeed in a predominantly male world. In assessing the situation, she accepted factors she could not control and manipulated factors she could. Mead realized she could more readily work as an anthropologist in an area in which women by tradition had staked a claim, an area men had no inclination to investigate. Hence, she readily agreed with Boas when he suggested she study children in a society. Plunging into an area of research dominated by men and trying to supplant them would have created multiple problems. Her reasoning not only led her to Samoa to study adolescent angst in 1925, but it also guided her decisions throughout her life in similar circumstances and provided the focus of her work.

As Margaret prepared to leave for Samoa, Luther was aware that an older colleague, Edward Sapir, was pursuing her. Sapir was a widower, eighteen years older than Mead, with three children. A protégé of Boas's and already a recognized authority in the field of linguistic anthropology, he was a close friend of Ruth Benedict, with whom he carried on a "voluminous correspondence" (Lapsley 1999: 65). Margaret was clearly enthralled with his attention and his intellect. Sapir, however, tried to persuade Boas that Margaret's health was not equal to the rigors of a year in a tropical climate. Margaret resented Sapir's interference, especially the implied sexism, and no matter how enraptured, she surely had no desire to divorce and tie herself down with rearing Sapir's children. Despite the attentions of Sapir, Margaret was consumed during the summer of 1925 with planning her trip while Luther wrapped up his responsibilities and prepared to begin a year's fellowship in England.

Luther's recollection of one of the best weeks of their marriage was the week before Margaret left for Samoa. The small, plain cottage on Narragansett Bay, Rhode Island, offered a welcome retreat from the tensions of the previous two years. The week passed quickly and soon it was time for Margaret to leave on her long journey to the group of Pacific islands known collectively as Oceania, an area that would soon become synonymous with the name Margaret Mead in the American psyche. Even Mead herself could not have realized that her decision to conduct her initial fieldwork on the Samoan island of Ta'u would be such a choice point in her life.

Chapter 3

TA'U, TARO, AND TALKING CHIEFS (1925–1926)

> A knowledge of one other culture should sharpen our
> ability to scrutinize more steadily, to appreciate more
> lovingly, our own.
> —Mead, *Coming of Age in Samoa* (1961)

The Mead family enjoyed a lively dinner at their Bucks County, Pennsylvania, farmhouse, and then the entire entourage drove Margaret to the old Baltimore & Ohio train station in Philadelphia. Dusk and dirt combined to add to the sense of sadness felt by her family. Many years later Luther remembered the filth of the train station mixed with the gloom of their little group. Luther hugged and kissed Margaret and stepped back to allow her family their goodbyes. She kissed each one and, alone, walked through a gate to board the train and begin her long journey to Samoa.

Mead wrote in her autobiography that her father later commented, "She never looked back!" (1972: 13). A children's book about her was titled *She Never Looked Back* (Epstein and Epstein 1980) and numerous biographers have mentioned her father's comment, presumably because the vignette illustrates her lack of fear of the unknown adventures that awaited her.[1]

Luther's account of Margaret's leaving for Samoa is more traditional. He wrote that after she climbed aboard, she turned "and waved to us from the platform" (Cressman 1988: 131). Even if Margaret made a symbolically visible sign of looking back, in actuality she did not waver in moving forward on a potentially dangerous adventure. This slightly built young woman, not yet twenty-four years old, was embarking on a trip halfway around the world. She

51

would spend almost a year working with culturally different people whose complex language she did not yet speak, in an era in which long-distance communication was limited to brief messages by wire or slow letters by ship.

ESTRANGEMENT FROM CRESSMAN

When Luther sailed for England, he carried many apprehensions about whether he and Margaret would reunite in France the next summer as planned. And with good reason. Before he left, Luther received his first letter from Margaret, mailed from San Francisco. Cressman was unprepared for what he read. Despite Margaret's being very absorbed in advancing her career, despite both of them carrying loads as full-time students along with part-time jobs, despite little time and energy to devote to nurturing a marriage, and despite the attentions of Edward Sapir, Luther was surprised at the letter's brief and puzzling contents. She told him she would leave him only if she fell in love with someone else. Even the mild-mannered Luther, who certainly encouraged Margaret to follow her own desires, could not be expected to shrug off such a letter.

In writing their separate autobiographies, Margaret and Luther differed over a variety of points about their nearly six years of engagement and five years of marriage. In *A Golden Journey*, Cressman, who had the advantage of being aware of what she had written, commended Margaret for her ability to have a global view of events and the talent to write about them in a readable way, but he insisted that in matters of dates and facts, his is the correct recollection. "Margaret, a historian?" he wrote, "NO! A dramatist? OUTSTANDING!" (1988: 128). He wrote that his own perception of events was not intended to attack her, but he felt Margaret's autobiography was written "in a terrible hurry, 'off the top of her head'" (1988: 195). Mead herself acknowledged that she wrote *Blackberry Winter* in ten weeks.

The Cressman-Mead marriage probably started to unravel the day it began. While a childhood dream of Margaret's had been to marry an Episcopal priest and rear a large family, after marriage she never made an effort to attend services with Luther, and when Luther's small church in Brooklyn hosted a reception to welcome them as priest and wife, she was uncomfortable interacting with the congregation. "Although Margaret tried hard to fit into her position, she was ill at ease, a feeling obviously experienced by all. That single experience was another significant portent" (Cressman 1988: 193).

Luther's concerns went deeper, however, than Mead's alienation from his congregation. He was distancing himself from the church as his work at Columbia gave him new insights that caused him to question the unconditional acceptance of church doctrine. He was also disillusioned with American society in general and with the changes he saw in society's values, values that he and other young men like him had risked and in many cases had given their lives to preserve.

Luther was disappointed that Margaret was not a sympathetic listener to his concerns and may have tended to keep problems to himself because he recognized the marriage could not withstand being twisted in too many directions. Despite the reasons, Margaret did not see, or perhaps did not want to see, difficulties in the marriage. She felt she had the marriage she wanted, one that was better than her mother's, with both a supportive husband and a career, "a marriage in which there seemed to be no obstacles to being myself" (Mead 1972: 133).

And so Luther left for his own year abroad, seeking peace within himself, feeling disillusionment with his profession, and sensing the questionable future of his marriage. Little wonder that half a century later Cressman remembered that he felt "engulfed by a sense of aloneness in a world that didn't care" (1988: 134) while on the ship that would take him across the Atlantic.

SIDE TRIPS

Mead did not travel from Philadelphia to Samoa alone, as she implied in *Blackberry Winter*. Ruth Benedict joined her and they traveled together to Arizona. Reflecting on the impressive beauty of the Grand Canyon, Mead wrote her grandmother, "the part I loved the best was the endless possibilities of those miles of pinnacled clay, red and white, and fantastic, ever changing their aspect under a new shadowing cloud" (as cited in Lapsley 1999: 124).

Mead and Benedict used their unhurried time together to reconcile personal difficulties. Edward Sapir had also charmed Ruth and she was devastated when she found that Sapir and Margaret were romantically involved with each other. Mead's daughter, Mary Catherine Bateson, wrote in her memoirs, *With a Daughter's Eye*, "Ruth and Margaret decided that neither of them would choose further intimacy with Sapir, but rather preferred each other" (1984: 151). Margaret described this resolution to close friend Marie Eichelberger, who many years later told Bateson how they had used the immediacy of the Sapir situation to arrive at a new intimacy with each other, "sitting and overlooking the Grand Canyon" (Bateson 1984: 151).

Hilary Lapsley, in *Margaret Mead and Ruth Benedict: The Kinship of Women*, presents a convincing case and extensive documentation for a lesbian relationship between Mead and Benedict and states, "Sometime in 1923 or 1924, after Margaret graduated from college, she and Ruth became lovers. 'Almost imperceptibly, our relationship became one of colleagues and close friends,' Margaret recalled, omitting to mention, in the interests of secrecy, this other transition" (1999: 75). (See chapter 8 for a more complete description of the Mead-Benedict relationship.)

In addition to her short personal visit to the Grand Canyon with Ruth, Margaret made several professional stops en route to Samoa. An especially fruitful stop was in Honolulu, where college friends of her mother's provided contacts and made arrangements to ensure her time was well spent. She was treated as a member of the staff at the Bishop Museum and received lessons in a Polynesian language similar to Samoan. May Dillingham Freer, or Mother May as Margaret called her mother's friend, gave her a small silk pillow after a biologist told Mead that if she always carried a little pillow with her she could lie on anything. Mead considered this one of the few bits of practical advice she received, a detail that sadly shows how sorely practical advice was needed. Her two weeks in Honolulu were a profitable and positive start to long months in the field.

PAGO PAGO

Mead's ship docked in the harbor of Pago Pago (pronounced "Pango Pango") on August 31, 1925. She was now 7,200 miles from New York and her best access to home was via letters brought by ship every three weeks.

Pago Pago, the capital, is on Tutuila, one of the main islands that, with several smaller ones, make up the archipelago recognized since 1900 as American Samoa. Sixty miles east of Tutuila are the three islands of Ta'u, Ofu, and Olosenga, collectively known as Manu'a and considered to be the birthplace of Polynesia, since language and artifacts indicate a Polynesian culture that originated there over 3,000 years ago and then spread across the Pacific.

Margaret made her way to a hotel immortalized in a 1921 Somerset Maugham story and play, *Rain*, which Margaret had seen performed in New York. Age had removed any glamour associated with the hotel's past. Margaret was forced to eat meals poorly prepared by the hotel cook, Fa'alavelave, whose translated name was symbolic of his culinary skills—"Misfortune."

Mead was eager to begin work investigating whether Samoan females experience the same stress during adolescence that American females experience; however, because the National Research Council insisted on mailing money to her rather than entrusting her to carry it, she could not pay her bill and leave the hotel until the ship arrived with her grant money. Cressman noted in his 1988 autobiography that Mead traveled "under financial conditions a contemporary graduate student would probably reject as demeaning" (Cressman 1888: 493–94). Although she was forced to endure six long weeks as the hotel's resident boarder, Mead preferred to maintain the independence she would have lost had she lived in a private home.

While waiting, Mead occupied her time learning to speak Samoan. She was helped immensely by a letter from an old friend of her father-in-law's. As the current surgeon general of the US Navy, the friend was delighted to repay Luther's father for a favor done many years previously by giving Margaret a letter of introduction and instructing navy personnel in Samoa to assist her. How pleased, Luther noted almost sixty years later in his autobiography, his father would have been to read Margaret's grateful acknowledgment of his help in *Blackberry Winter*. Because of the surgeon general's support, the chief nurse of the navy's medical department assigned a young Samoan nurse who spoke excellent English to tutor Margaret in the Samoan language one hour a day. Mead spent another seven hours memorizing vocabulary.

Some anthropologists later questioned the results of Mead's work because they doubted she was able to pick up the nuances of the Samoan language, considered the most archaic of the Polynesian tongues and a very difficult language to master. Although throughout her life Mead never showed a real strength in mastering new languages, letters to Boas verify she sought out people with whom she could converse and confirm that she had learned to speak adequately enough to interview the Samoan girls in their native language. By mid-September 1925 she wrote that she was able to speak Samoan better than she could understand it spoken. Several times a week she visited the home of the principal of the government school and his wife to chat casually. In October she wrote that learning the language was going more slowly but that she was still taking lessons and afterward would try to find someone with whom she could carry on a conversation. By mid-November Mead reported to Boas that she was able to work with informants who did not speak English and that she could make speeches, when necessary, in Samoan.

Mead also spent time steeping herself in the customs and culture of the country. She visited every village on the island of Tutuila. One visit was to the home of a woman whose mother was a full-blooded Samoan of noble birth. Mrs. Wilson, the daughter, was an intelligent woman who had been educated in Honolulu and whose social skills in both cultures were impeccable. While eating a luncheon of roast chicken spread out on banana leaves, Mrs. Wilson described Samoan customs. Her mother, who Margaret wrote was the originator of colored tapa cloth (made from tree bark that is scraped and pounded), confirmed questionable points. Mrs. Wilson also talked about her life when her husband, then a navy captain, was stationed in Michigan, where she was called "squaw" and "a brown thing." "Her feelings," Mead wrote, "are raw and bleeding under insults from white people" (1977: 27).

TEN DAYS WITH A LOCAL CHIEF

From October 19 to October 28, 1925, after finally escaping from the hotel in Pago Pago, Mead lived for ten days with a chief, Ufuti, and his family in the village of Vaitogi, three miles from a bus line and many leagues from Western-style life. Daughter Fa'amotu was both a friend and a tutor in Samoan culture and etiquette, and other members of the household, including two *tulafales*, or talking chiefs, served as "official orators, spokesmen and ambassadors of chiefs" (Mead 1961a: 39). These talking chiefs, named Lolo and Ofoio, also mentored Mead.

At last, Mead could practice the Samoan customs and habits that she had primarily heard about. She learned to bathe by wearing a saronglike outfit in the village shower and then, in full view of staring eyes, changing to a dry one. She learned to eat Samoan food; although she enjoyed many dishes, especially chicken and fruits like mangoes, bananas, and papayas, she described the starchy taro root as tasteless. She wrote in an October 13 letter that she ate native food but that it was too starchy for her primary diet. Also, as a guest, she initially felt on display when the others waited for her to eat before they began.

Gradually, as the ten days passed, she was better able to sit for long periods with legs crossed, dance, relate to the Samoans, and feel comfortable speaking their language. In fact, she made a flowery farewell speech, as was expected of her, in Samoan. Giving such speeches to an assembled group, she wrote, in a language in which a slight rise or fall in intonation changed meaning, was difficult, especially with her host family invested in her success.

Mead's acceptance in Vaitogi was cemented when Ufuti bestowed upon her the first of three honorary titles of *taupou* that she received while in Samoa, to indicate she was a maiden, or virgin, of high rank, possible because she kept her marriage secret. To Mead, revealing her marital status seemed risky and might have raised questions and erected barriers to her work, since a married woman traveling alone was considered extremely improper in the 1920s. Because she was a slim ninety-eight pounds, stood only five feet, two and a half inches high, and looked no older than the tall, well-developed Samoan adolescents she came to study, people assumed she was unmarried, a perception Mead did not correct.

THE ISLAND OF TA'U

Mead realized that living in the sheltered home of a chieftain in which she held an exalted status, as in the village of Vaitogi, would adversely affect the results of her research by limiting interactions with the young girls she planned to study. She returned to Pago Pago to gather her belongings and leave for the island of Ta'u in the Manu'a group. Ta'u, an island of about eight by eleven miles, had four villages, three within easy walking distance, and was removed by both culture and distance from Tutuila. On November 14, 1925, Mead reported in a letter that she anticipated living in Ta'u until she returned home, as it was an excellent location to carry out her research.

Mead's detractors have attacked her for living in the household of the only white family on Ta'u, Navy Chief Pharmacist's Mate Edward R. Holt, his wife and two children, and two other navy men—Sparks, a radio operator who spent much of his time either toying with the radio or reading magazines about radio equipment, and Wiezorek, a sanitary inspector. The local pastor and political boss presented Mead with a young girl to be her companion, because she was assumed to be an unmarried woman and therefore was not to be seen alone. Felofiaina, who spoke no English, stayed with Mead during the day and helped count and survey the kin relationships among the villagers.

Living in half of the back porch of the dispensary gave Mead the privacy that a house among the villagers would not provide, since Samoan houses were both open air and open to all, with the latter including chickens, pigs, dogs, and cats as well as people. Privacy was important to Mead for several reasons. First, she needed a retreat in which to work, administer tests, and interview the adolescent girls, yet she could also push aside curtains and turn the entire porch into a communal area in which visitors, especially the young people, could gather to sing and dance. Second, from her own quarters she could wander through the village freely and chat with various people. If she lived with a village family, she would have seemed connected to them, although, as she pointed out in a letter to Boas, she would have benefited from practice in speaking the language. Living with the Holts seemed sensible to Mead, but she nevertheless expressed concern about her Westernized living arrangements in an October 11, 1925, letter to Ruth

Benedict, in which she wrote, "I don't know if I'm just coddling myself" (Library of Congress: b).

Her letter to Boas on November 29, 1925, presented a lengthy overview of her accomplishments thus far. She described the island of Ta'u, the villagers, the role of religion, the government school, her initial insights regarding adolescent girls, the missionary influence, contrasts between Samoan and American girls, and her justification for living in a white household. She noted that most Samoans are Christian and that native pastors choose some girls to live with them under close supervision. Mead also noted that she had not observed adolescent insubordination during the twenty days she had lived on Ta'u. She concluded by saying she would include information on the lack of insubordination in her National Research Council report, which would need to leave Samoa the first of January to arrive in New York by the March due date, but information about sex and religious matters would have to wait until she could better speak Samoan. As it turned out, that report was delayed until January 5. The stifling heat, described in an October 11 letter as diminishing her efficiency by half, was only one cause of her difficulties.

A SETBACK

The night of December 31, 1925, Mead joined the villagers in a rainy walk along the seashore, with horrendous noise from both an agitated sea and tin cans rattled by boys who wore them around their necks in celebration of the new year. On New Year's Day, 1926, ominous weather turned into a hurricane that flattened the entire village. Mead wrote that the driving rain was mixed with sand, coconuts, and pieces of tin from roofs.

Sparks, the sailor Mead had written condescendingly about a few short weeks before as having only a third-grade education and being more concerned with radios, joined Wiezorek in the pelting rain to hack into a cement water tank. After they made a hole to let the water out, Mead climbed down into the blackness of the tank and held up a tub in which Edward Holt placed his infant child. After the baby had been lowered within, Sparks, Wiezorek, and the rest of the Holt family followed into the safety of the tank. At last they settled into position in the approximately four-by-five-foot tank, with Margaret holding a roasted chicken, a large red candle, an electric candle and extra batteries, a loaf of bread, and a basin to catch rainwater that dripped from the tank's battered tin roof. Morning revealed that one of the few structures left standing was the dispensary.

In the 1920s, news, especially news about little-known Polynesian islands, did not travel so quickly and was not repeated so excessively by all manner of communication as today; however, within several days Mead's New York friends and colleagues read that Manu'a was especially hard hit by the horrific hurricane and cabled Mead, requesting a reply. Mead cabled Boas a terse "Well" on January 12, 1926. Boas phoned Benedict, who was much relieved and who in turn contacted the Mead family and various friends. Emily Mead wrote to Margaret, rebuking her. Since Margaret had said devastating hurricanes happened every ten years, she felt that Margaret knew there would be a hurricane and wrote that "you chose this year on purpose" (Mead 1977: 246).

A few days later Benedict herself received a cable from Mead, but Luther did not learn of the hurricane until a letter from Ruth arrived to tell him. The personal relationship between Luther and Margaret was now very different from the early days of their engagement, when Margaret daily wrote him four pages.

Mead spent several weeks helping the villagers put their lives and homes back in order. However, living among the Samoans did not help Mead discover answers to her primary research problem. In mid-January, when her stay in Samoa was half over, she was finally able to again investigate the problem she had traveled so far to answer: Is the period of adolescence less stressful among Samoan females than it is in the United States and other Western cultures?

NO ESTABLISHED PROTOCOLS OR PROCEDURES

Mead's coursework, heavy on theory, was light on the practicalities involved. "There was," she wrote, "no *how* in our education. What we learned was *what* to look for" (1972: 151).

Mead went to Samoa with limited supplies and equipment. Even clothing was an issue; in an era in which natural fibers were the only available choices, she took half a dozen cotton dresses after being advised that silk would rot, only to find that most navy women wore silk. For data collection and recordation, she took a strongbox to secure money and papers, a small camera, a portable typewriter, six notebooks, typing and carbon paper, and a flashlight. At a party on a stopover in Berkeley, California, a professor asked whether her equipment included a good lamp. She had not known or thought to include one with her equipment.

Just as no checklist of equipment and clothing existed, established procedures and protocols were yet to evolve. Nor did Boas pass on the practical information he and earlier anthropologists had gained from field experiences. Fred Eggan, an eminent anthropologist at the University of Chicago, referred to the "sink or swim" (1974: 9) procedures of the early 1920s.

Mead wrote in *Blackberry Winter* about the enormous responsibilities an anthropologist carries on an initial trip into the field in learning to understand the spoken language and to speak it, to recognize people and understand their body language spoken with glances, gestures, silence, and acts, and then to weave everything together into a composite picture of the culture. In addition, although all anthropologists must respond to individual circumstances, researching a little-studied culture complicated Mead's work. While in Samoa Mead herself questioned her techniques. She didn't know whether she was using the right methods. "What were the right methods? There were no precedents to fall back on" (1972: 163).

Certainly, Mead's childhood experiences assisted her as she set about collecting the information she needed to answer her research questions. Her father's practical rather than theoretical approach to understanding process taught her how to observe. Her mother's sociological technique taught Mead how to record her observations. Emily had endlessly documented myriad subjects useful in her work writing entries for encyclopedias and had kept voluminous notes about Margaret's birth and toddler years, enough to fill thirteen notebooks. Even when Mead accompanied her mother to a wedding, while the other women dabbed their eyes with joy, Emily furiously scribbled notes about the event.

As a child, Margaret had gained her own practical experience making and recording observations. Because Emily was less compulsive in taking notes about her younger children, Margaret took over and, with her grandmother Martha's help, described their stages of growth. So from her early years, Margaret had not only the model of her mother but also actual practice in observing, recording, and analyzing behavior.

Mead's training in psychology had taught her about tests and inventories useful to sample behavior and an aunt had shared examples of casework from her experiences at Hull House in Chicago, a settlement residence founded by social reformer Jane Addams to provide immigrants with daycare, job placement, and educational classes.

Mead considered herself very careful in both carrying out and reporting research because she believed her mother's study of Italian immigrants had forced the Mead family, who sensed the immigrants' indignation over being the objects of research, to move from one of Margaret's childhood homes. Throughout her life, Mead carefully and discreetly reported about the groups she studied, even if they did not read and write English, and she conscientiously disguised names and went to great lengths to protect her informants.

Martin Orans, an anthropologist who researched Mead's materials that now reside at the Library of Congress in Washington, DC, for his book *Not Even Wrong: Margaret Mead, Derek Freeman, and the Samoans*, credited Mead with preserving her notes. "It is to Mead's everlasting credit that she preserved her field materials so that they may be examined for scholarly purposes. Many anthropologists have confessed to me that they would never have had the courage to do so; the conjecture must surely be that these anthropologists have claimed more than was warranted by their observations" (1996: 17–18).

The style of fieldwork being developed in the 1920s and whose techniques Mead helped refine became known as participant observation. By definition, participant observation is self-explanatory; it involves learning the language and unobtrusively immersing oneself in all aspects of the culture in which one is conducting fieldwork. One of Mead's techniques entailed cultivating informants whom she could trust. While the word *informant* frequently has a negative connotation, for anthropologists the informant is crucial to obtaining valid, reliable information about the culture and language. In return, Mead gave these informants gifts; for example, paper, cigarettes, matches, needles and thread, and scissors.

The training early anthropologists received, while providing limited specifics about techniques, emphasized the uniqueness and value of all human beings and an obligation not to disrupt the society being studied. As Mead pointed out, their training taught them to respect the people they studied. In a 1973 article titled "Changing Styles of Anthropological Work," written for the *Annual Review of Anthropology*, Mead wrote almost longingly of those days of "trust and cooperation between an anthropologist and his informants, no matter how disparate their education, in which both were devoted to recording a vanishing culture and assuring the safety of its artifacts" (1973b: 16). Although trust and cooperation no doubt existed, during this classic era of anthropology most fieldwork was done in colonial possessions, like American Samoa, or on Native American reservations. Since the administrators of the region gave the required permission, the people studied had no choice and did not question the work of the anthropologists.

OBSERVATIONS OF SAMOAN FEMALES

Boas had specifically told Mead not to include ethnographic data; that is, she was not to scientifically study and document information about the culture as a whole. She was to focus only on adolescent girls. To study adolescents, however, Mead felt a need to collect information that would help her better understand the girls in the three nearby villages. She also turned the ethnographic information into a monograph, *Social Organization of Manu'a*, for the Bishop Museum in Honolulu.

Mead worked as many hours each day as possible, but she had no idea whether she was using methods that would produce the kind of results Boas and the National Research Council wanted. She took a census of the villages. She drew a schematic that showed houses. She observed and gathered information about kin relationships, family positions, and wealth. She danced and ate and talked. She sat with bare feet and crossed legs for hours while listening to formal speeches and informal conversations. She kept her living quarters on the porch open from early morning until late night so she could mingle with young people and learn from them. Then, pulling from her background in psychology and sociology as well as anthropology, she crafted tests, developed interview questions and a questionnaire, analyzed family structure, and wrote case histories.

Mead collected data on girls between the approximate ages of eight and twenty. The number varies from fifty to seventy, depending on how one counts the girls she intensively interviewed and those with whom she had fewer interactions. Birth, especially among people of high rank, was an important event, but age was arbitrary in Samoa and even mothers remembered only birth order, not the birth date and actual age of their children, so Mead classified the girls as "adolescent," "just reaching puberty," and "preadolescent." Regardless of the exact number of subjects she studied, Mead noted that, given approximately 600 villagers, the number of girls in her sample population was a proportionately high enough number when compared to the total population to ensure valid results. Mead added that the limited number of subjects was further validated by the small number of exceptions she found; that is, in a simple society like Samoa the similarity of experiences of the girls enabled her to generalize even though only fifty girls in three villages were studied.

MEAD'S CONCLUSIONS

Mead concluded that Samoan young women do not suffer the stress felt by young women in the Western world because, while physically females go through the same bodily changes, a less complex Samoan society results in less storm and stress in their lives. Children growing up in Samoan society lived a very different life, Mead found, from children in the United States. Preadolescent girls from about age six or seven were given huge responsibilities. They tended the babies and toddlers, developing such daily living skills as toilet training and keeping the younger children both out of harm and out of mischief. They ran errands and did small chores, like lighting lamps and fetching items adults wanted. Mead also marveled that children age fourteen and under perform the "irritating, detailed routine of housekeeping, which in our civilisation is accused of warping the souls and souring the tempers of grown women" (1961a: 28). As they neared puberty, if they were strong and healthy, girls worked on the coconut plantations with their parents, went on fishing expeditions, and learned more complex household skills, including making bark cloth and weaving baskets, fans, floor mats, and blinds.

After their essential training was completed, the girls, now adolescents, continued to work but had limited responsibilities until marriage, when presumably the cycle began again with the birth of their own children. Mead decided that, for Samoan females, the adolescent years were the best period in life, with time and freedom to enjoy one's self. While sexual activity was not obligatory for young women, neither was it discouraged, except for those who lived in the missionary boarding school or who were daughters of ranking chiefs. Obviously, Mead reasoned, the Samoan young woman does not go through the stormy period weathered by young women in Western societies. By extension, the storm of adolescence is a cultural construction rather than a biological inevitability akin to losing one's baby teeth.

Much of Mead's information was derived from investigation into her research problem, but by speaking Samoan and living among the people Mead also experienced events that outsiders might easily envy. She shared her adventures in *Coming of Age in Samoa*, originally published in 1928, in which readers can vicariously visit Manu'a. Mead's vivid prose allows a reader to imagine receiving shell and seed necklaces at Christmas, fishing and crabbing by torchlight, watching girls return from bathing in the sea, their wet lavalavas tied as sarongs and seeing boys dance and play guitars and ukuleles far into the night, their chests oiled and their faces painted with red and blue beards and mustaches.

RETURN FROM OCEANIA

Toward the end of Mead's sojourn in Samoa, one issue no longer muddied the Cressman-Mead relationship. When Edward Sapir wrote to Mead to tell her he was in love with someone receptive to caring for him and his children, Margaret made a fire on the beach and burned his letters. She had planned, and undoubtedly preferred, to be the rejecter rather than the rejectee. Given that throughout her entire life Mead saved every scrap of paper either written or received, one can easily imagine her fury. Her anger was undoubtedly rekindled upon recalling his severe criticism, later recanted, of her poetry. This incident is thoroughly described in Lapsley (111) who discusses a letter Sapir wrote on February 14, 1925, telling Ruth Benedict that he had been critical of Margaret's poetry when he had written to her the previous day. (See chapter 7 for another incident in which she destroyed documents.)

In the spring of 1926 Mead wrapped up her work in Samoa, returned to Pago Pago, and set sail for Sydney, Australia, to begin a slow six-week voyage to France, where she would rejoin Luther. The date she actually left is not clear. In *Blackberry Winter* she says she left in June, and information in *Coming of Age in Samoa* is confusing, but "the evidence suggests that she left Ta'u in mid-April and Pago Pago at the end of April or early May" (Lapsley 1999: 321). The length of her total stay in Samoa was approximately eight to nine months; she lived with the Holts about four months. Mead was probably consciously ambiguous because of criticism that the time frame was too short for her to collect meaningful data.

Luther, also concluding his year of study abroad, was eager to show Margaret, on her first trip to Europe, some of the most beautiful areas in the south of France. If he also hoped the year's separation would increase Margaret's love for him, he was mistaken. That seemed improbable and fate intervened on Margaret's return trip from Samoa to make it impossible.

Chapter 4

PEOPLE ARE MADE, NOT BORN (1926–1929)

> In following the steps by which the infant learns his civilization, we are tracing a process of transmission, not one of creation; but the path is none the less revealing.
> —Mead, *Male and Female*, 61

Mead met Reo (pronounced "Ray-o") Franklin Fortune, a psychologist from New Zealand, when the SS *Chitral* docked in Sydney, Australia, in late spring, 1926. The intellectual atmosphere of Columbia University was almost a year in the past and, with a tedious and tiresome trip stretching weeks into the future, Mead was open to a relationship with the charming, erudite Reo.

Reo was fifteen months younger than Margaret. His father left the missionary life to dairy farm in New Zealand with only a few pounds in the family's collective pockets, a career change that did not make Reo's obtaining advanced education easy. Nevertheless, his intelligence and astuteness in learning languages helped him earn a BA in advanced philosophy. When the blue-eyed, tall, dark-haired graduate student met Mead, he was on his way to study at Cambridge University, England, as the recipient of a fellowship earned by his master's thesis on dreams, a topic he had begun to research as an undergraduate. A young woman named Eileen had recently shattered a different kind of dream—that of marriage.

From the beginning of their relationship, Reo influenced Margaret to record her dreams and stimulated a lifelong interest in their meaning. Between the time of her July 1928 divorce from Luther and her October 1928 marriage to Reo, she lived with college friends, one of whom, Léonie Adams, told Margaret that dreams were the basis of some of her poems. Interest in dreams persisted throughout Mead's life, and years later she placed an easel by the bed of her daughter so Cathy could draw pictures of what she dreamed immediately upon arising.

AN EMOTIONAL FIRST VISIT TO EUROPE

The trip from Sydney to Marseilles, France, took seven weeks, ample time for Margaret and Reo to share many personal and professional experiences. Mead wrote in her autobiography that one of her few regrets in life was lingering aboard to talk with Reo when the ship docked in Marseilles in the summer of 1926. Luther, awaiting her arrival, was "almost ill with disappointment and fear that something had happened to Margaret" (Cressman 1988: 176). She greeted her husband without any enthusiasm, according to Luther, saying only that she had been talking and didn't notice the ship had docked. When they reached their hotel room, Margaret soon told him about Reo. One would assume Margaret quickly left Luther when she fell in love with another man. Reality is not quite so tidy. Several years would pass before matters were sorted out.

A former student and longtime friend of Mead's once complained to her that she had left out the interesting tidbits about her marriages and talked blandly around the men in her life in *Blackberry Winter*. The complaint was valid. Mead's autobiography catalogs events and speaks in generalities more than it reveals feelings. She doesn't divulge her state of mind when she recognized that her feelings for Reo were growing. She did say that other passengers assumed she and Reo were having an affair because they were so involved with each other aboard the *Chitral*. They were not having an affair, she added, but they were falling in love (Mead 1972: 174).

Margaret and Luther toured France with Barnard College friend Louise Rosenblatt, and he and Margaret talked constantly about the perplexity of their situation. In his memoirs, Luther wrote that Margaret clearly was in love with Reo but was unsure if the situation could work out or should remain a fantasy. Luther had resolved his own personal problems and decided to leave the priesthood. In his memoirs, Luther credited Boas with helping to resolve the difficulties he carried with him to Europe and wrote that Boas had introduced him to an intellectual world that provided the means for him to analyze problems and rationally and responsibly solve them. Luther felt that Margaret must sort out her own life issues, as he had.

When they were in Paris, Margaret received a letter from Reo. He had continued on to England but then romantically planned a return visit to Margaret. Luther, knowing that Fortune's arrival at their hotel was imminent, tried to absent himself but accidentally ran into Reo in the hotel lobby. Both Reo and the concierge behind the desk were speechless when Luther agreeably introduced himself in English to Reo, told the concierge in French that Margaret was expecting a visitor and then, again in English, directed Reo to their room. In another encounter, when Luther saw Reo and Margaret locked in an embrace, he disappeared into the shadows. Confrontation was not his style, and he wanted Margaret as his wife only if she freely made that choice.

Although Luther's modus operandi was not to control, and although he believed that love could not be demanded or forced, friendship with Dorothy Cecelia Loch, a British friend of an American friend, no doubt offered some relief from his pain. Loch, English by birth, Scots by a long line of distinguished ancestors, shared common interests with Luther, although she was nine years older than he. She had worked at the British Sociological Society and helped Luther make important contacts during the year of his fellowship. He noted in his memoirs that he and Dorothy agreed not to mention romance until he and Margaret had put their lives in order, an event that was deferred over a year, until August 1927.

RETURN TO NEW YORK CITY

Luther was delighted to receive an offer to return to his previous position teaching sociology at the College of the City of New York, whose name became City College (CCNY) in 1929. It was a position he much desired and gave him an excuse for returning to New York early and leaving personal tensions and entanglements in Europe.

In *Blackberry Winter*, Margaret wrote simply that he had to return home to prepare for teaching. Luther related that, as he prepared to board the train en route to his ship, Margaret began to cry and begged him to tell her what to do. He told her she must make her own decision and, as he stepped onto the train, he saw his young wife crying into friend Louise's shoulder and called, "Take care of her, Louise, take care of her!" (Cressman 1988: 181).

Margaret toured Rome with Benedict and then attended the Congress of Americanists. In the year they had been separated, Ruth had taken on a middle-aged beauty and seemed to have gained a self-confidence previously lacking. She was a gracefully tall woman with expressive eyes and her drab brown hair, now cut and prematurely gray, formed a striking silver coif that framed her face. As for Reo, Margaret was unable to reunite with him in Paris because of a blocked railroad tunnel. They finally did meet and in September he saw her off on the ship that would carry her and Ruth home.

Ten days later, when the ship docked in New York, Margaret was greeted by the Ash Can Cats and Luther. The autumn of 1926 began, and Margaret and Luther slipped into the routines of life. They settled into their apartment and into their jobs, Luther as a professor in the Department of Government at CCNY while also writing scholarly articles, and Margaret as assistant curator of ethnology at the American Museum of Natural History, her first full-time job, while also analyzing and compiling material on her Samoan fieldwork.

In the 1920s, much discrimination existed against professional women; they had limited career opportunities no matter how remarkable their résumés. Mead had accepted, with Boas's recommendation, the position as assistant curator the summer before. Although the American Museum of Natural History was one of the country's premier museums, Mead's position was not nearly so prestigious as a faculty position with a university; her connection with the museum, however, continued until her death more than fifty years later.

WRITING *COMING OF AGE IN SAMOA*

In her 1911 diary, ten-year-old Margaret had written, "I'm going to just sort of tell a story, and say what I think about things, and people"

(Library of Congress: d). In fact, that characteristic of her writing made her book about her Samoan adventures a best-seller and also led to later criticism.

"As the dawn begins to fall among the soft brown roofs and the slender palm trees stand out against a colourless, gleaming sea, lovers slip home from trysts beneath the palm trees or in the shadow of beached canoes, that the light may find each sleeper in his appointed place" (Mead 1961a: 14). Thus began *Coming of Age in Samoa*.

Mead's use of poetic language to describe a part of the world with which few were familiar captured the imagination of her readers and, while not considered risqué today, was more sexually suggestive than material read by the average person in the late 1920s and early 1930s. Anthropologists have since questioned whether the Samoa of the 1920s was the idyllic paradise Mead described, but the sensual images, combined with vivid and visual language very different from books written by academics, captured the imagination of the public. Little wonder that, since its first appearance in bookstores in 1928, it has been published in sixteen languages and continues to sell.

After introducing the reader to the start of an average Samoan day, Mead described the villagers eating breakfast and going to their morning's work. She continued: "It is high noon. The sand burns the feet of the little children, who leave their palm leaf balls and their pinwheels of frangipani blossoms to wither in the sun, as they creep into the shade of the houses" (16). Mead ended the chapter by saying, "Sometimes sleep will not descend upon the village until long past midnight; then at last there is only the mellow thunder of the reef and the whisper of lovers, as the village rests until dawn" (19).

From Pen to Print

In 1926, George Dorsey, an ethnologist turned successful writer, recommended Margaret send the manuscript to the publishing house of Harper & Brothers. Dorsey also suggested "Coming of Age in Samoa" as the title of the book. When Harper rejected the manuscript, Dorsey luckily maintained his interest in its publication and persuaded a man named William Morrow, who had recently started a publishing house, to consider it.

After reviewing the manuscript, Morrow brilliantly suggested to Mead that she add some material comparing Samoan with American adolescence. Mead readily agreed and in fact was well prepared to write the additional chapters. She had been relating her Samoan experiences to all types of audiences since she returned, noting the questions people asked and thinking through her responses. Morrow thus introduced the opportunity for Mead to make the right choice at another crucial juncture in her life, because the resulting final two chapters not only produced a bestseller but provided a springboard for a career in public speaking.

In an ironic aside, HarperCollins bought the William Morrow publishing house in 1999 and the 2001 reissue of Coming of Age in Samoa, timed to celebrate the centennial year of Mead's birth, was published by Harper Perennial.

Applying the Lessons of Samoa to America

Although Samoan society may not have been the pastoral paradise represented by Mead, it no doubt lacked the intensity of life in the United States. Mead discussed the tradeoffs with insight and honesty. The matter of choices impacted every aspect of life for American young people, she wrote. In matters of sex, single people in the 1920s were faced with various standards of morality, from marriage to variations of living together for a trial period with or without a commitment. By contrast, Samoan society in the 1920s was a casual society, she pointed out, and even if such a society did not create great leaders and great works of art, neither did it create teens with deep feelings about the multiple choices in their lives, choices that caused them to act in rebellious ways toward adults.

Choices, Mead wrote, were not limited to sexual matters in society in the United States. Choices permeated every aspect of the lives of Americans and came with many contradictions, based on race and diversity of background. To explain such conflict in the lives of Americans, Mead recommended that Americans compare a simple society in which change is slow with a modern society in which change is rapid. Mead also attributed the lack of neuroses among Samoans to a lack of demands made upon individuals, a situation far different from American society.

Mead ended the chapter "Our Educational Problems" by suggesting that Americans realize that a people are not predestined to act in a particular way but do so based on their history. She realized that American society was complex in the 1920s and so she did not advocate simplifying and modifying it to replicate Samoan society as a solution to social problems in the United States. She simply suggested that Americans consider other cultures in seeking solutions.

In the last chapter of *Coming of Age in Samoa*, Mead addressed the myriad choices available to young people, especially young females, in American society. Should Americans try to emulate the Samoans by limiting the choices available? No, wrote Mead, Americans need to teach children how to deal with the choices in life that they will have to make. She concluded the book by stating that in Samoa children learn a single way of life and then asked whether Americans, who know many different lifestyles, will allow their children to make their own choices. Her question is still valid in twenty-first-century America.

A TURN OF FORTUNE

Reo Fortune was unhappily settled on the opposite side of the Atlantic, in Cambridge, but he hoped a grant through A. R. Radcliffe-Brown's program at the University of Sydney would allow him to move from the field of psychology to anthropology and conduct fieldwork in New Guinea. He and Margaret carried on a correspondence that included, according to Mead, poetry.

Luther and Dorothy Loch, separated by that same ocean, continued to correspond with each other, but Luther wrote, his tone icy half a century later, that while Margaret was aware of the arrival of Dorothy's letters addressed to their apartment, "Reo's, I suppose, went to Margaret's museum address, for I have no memory of them arriving in the morning's mail at our apartment" (Cressman 1988: 190).

Margaret again sailed to Europe during the summer of 1927, ostensibly to visit museums and meet with European scholars in Oceanic cultures, but also, as Luther was aware, to meet Reo. Even so, Luther felt that a letter, written aboard ship and posted when she arrived in Hamburg, confirmed her commitment to their marriage. She wrote about their renting a new apartment and possibly traveling to France the next summer. Then, only a few days later, Luther received a short letter in which Margaret stated she wanted a divorce, a theme she echoed on her return to New York at the end of summer.

Luther moved to an apartment in Greenwich Village on August 27, 1927, and made plans for his own trip across the Atlantic, this time without a chafing marital attachment to irritate a relationship with Dorothy. Mead, with Luther's consent, filed for divorce in Hermosillo, Sonora, Mexico, where the grounds for divorce, unlike in New York, which mandated grounds of adultery, were more tolerant. The decree would become final in 1928.

THE IMPORTANCE OF MARRIAGE TO CRESSMAN

For the rest of his life, Luther remained puzzled about aspects of his marriage to Margaret and confused as to the depth and nature of her love for him. Cressman felt deeply that their marriage was important, that she was instrumental in shaping his life during the 1920s, and that he in turn shaped hers. In *A Golden Journey* he wrote that he provided support during the early years of her career and helped her believe in herself and make difficult decisions.

Mead later downplayed her first marriage and persisted in later years to call theirs a "student marriage" (1972: 316) and Luther a "student husband" (1977: 19). These terms bothered Cressman because they sounded as though the marriage had been undertaken with the idea that it was temporary. He and Margaret had, he felt, both exchanged vows with a hope for permanence in their relationship, despite Margaret's awareness that Luther felt divorce was appropriate if love disappeared from a marriage, a feeling with which she seemed to concur.

Mead justified saying little about their marriage in *Blackberry Winter* since "neither a book nor a child" (1972: 316) came out of their union. Thus, she reasoned, the marriage should remain private. Although Mead put "book" before "child," Cressman reversed this order in his 1988 autobiography and noted that this was her interpretation and that he did not consider the two equal achievements. Cressman described Mead as "lovely, not beautiful, young woman, my wife, willful at times, stubborn, sometimes quixotic, never simple, brilliant, goal-oriented and her course laid out, not permitting any interference with her steady progress in that direction, with an absorption in her work to which everything else had to be secondary in the long run" (131). More succinctly, Hilary Lapsley, in *Margaret Mead and Ruth Benedict: The Kinship of Women*, summarized Mead's personal choices in life by writing, "On a practical level, Margaret's primary loyalty was to her career" (1999: 93).

Luther later moved into archaeology (one of the four generally recognized fields within anthropology) at the suggestion of Benedict, and achieved recognition for founding the Oregon State Museum of Anthropology and the Department of Anthropology at the University of Oregon. In 1938 he excavated what came to be called the "Fort Rock sandals" from Fort Rock Cave in central Oregon. The sandals, later determined to date back approximately 9,000 years were an outstanding contribution to the field of archaeology.

The Cressman-Mead marriage was formally dissolved July 31, 1928, after five years of marriage. Cressman described the divorce as lacking bitterness but painful. He immediately left for England and Dorothy Loch. In recognition of starting a new life together, the couple decided to use middle names, so on August 31, 1928, Sheeleigh and Cecelia Cressman embarked on a union that lasted almost fifty years.

In late October 1979, Cressman's daughter, Gem, took her father to visit Margaret's grave at Trinity Episcopal Church, in Buckingham, Pennsylvania. He and Gem left roses and Luther whispered, "Shalom, dear Margaret, Shalom." With the Hebrew word meaning both "peace" and "goodbye" he felt that "the circle was now closed" (Cressman 1988: 200).

A DIFFERENT CIRCLE

Although Mead undertook her initial trip to Samoa alone, all of her subsequent fieldwork involved travel and research with at least one other anthropologist. On her second trip, the anthropologist was her second husband, Reo Fortune. On this venture, Mead had decided not to limit herself to adolescent and preadolescent girls but to study young children. She still planned to study a preliterate or so-called primitive society. Her choice of problem would revolve around mental development in young children. Specifically, she would investigate animistic thinking: Do children in a preliterate society attribute spiritual qualities to objects?

The decision of a location and a people with whom to work remained. Mead felt that she could investigate her problem anywhere within Melanesia, that area of the Pacific that lies northeast of Australia, and since Reo was already on the island of Dobu, now part of Papua New Guinea, finding a specific location for their work was left to him. Through a number of inquiries and his work with Radcliffe-Brown, Fortune decided on Manus, an island within the Admiralty group of the Bismarck Archipelago and now a province of Papua New Guinea, for their fieldwork. Margaret received funding and permission to take a year's leave from the American Museum of Natural History and left to meet her fiancé.

When her ship docked in Auckland, New Zealand, on October 8, 1928, Reo, fearing a change of mind on Margaret's part, impetuously announced he wanted to marry her that very day. After a great deal of rushing to have a ring made smaller, they dashed to the registry office and back to the ship, minutes before it set sail for Sydney.

When they arrived in Rabaul, the capital city of New Britain Island, then a territory of Australia, the government anthropologist assigned a young man named Banyalo to assist them. Banyalo was originally from the village of Pere on Manus Island. After Reo enlisted the help of another young man, Manuwai, also from Pere, Fortune and Mead selected that village in which to establish themselves.

Language was again a concern. Since they preferred not to work entirely through an interpreter, they had to concurrently learn Manus and pidgin English, later called Neo-Melanesian and then Tok Pisin, an

English-based compromise of various native tongues coupled with words derived from English. Some words are reasonably obvious; for example, *cook-boy* and *fashion-belong-white-man* (the ways of Europeans) (Mead 1977: 64). Others, like *longlong* (crazy), are obscure to the speaker of English. Mead appreciated the use of what was then called pidgin English as a lingua franca, or common language, because it provided an equal ground for native and foreign speakers, since both could speak the language equally well and communication difficulties were minimized. The language problem was complicated, however, by Banyalo's sulky reluctance to help Mead and Fortune learn either language.

While in Samoa Mead had begun duplicating and sending lengthy, informative letters to a group of friends and family members. She continued this lifelong practice when she wrote on December 16, 1928, soon after arriving, that Manus was a very difficult tongue to master: "hard phonetics, a mass of sounds which are intermediate between sounds familiar to us and a great deal of individual variation" (1977: 71). She went on to say that even within the village there were differences in the manner in which people pronounced the same word and attempts to negotiate an alternative pronunciation were ignored. She felt such variations made the Manus tongue much more difficult to learn than the Samoan.

Despite problems with language, she concluded that the village was beautiful and that the people had a culture and economic life that would make her and Fortune's stay productive. Indeed, Manus was so congenial that Mead returned there throughout her life.

Their reactions to the people of Manus were initially based on their former field experiences. Reo found the Manus people pleasant compared to the Dobuans, who were suspicious of each other. Mead was surprised to learn that, compared to the Samoans, the Manus were more materialistic, with much bartering and exchanging of local currency and goods. They were also very reliant on pleasing ghosts, who they believed freely punished them for large and small misdemeanors.

Part of their pleasure of the Pere location derived from the ambiance of the village. The approximately forty houses, built on stilts over water, had thatched roofs and an airiness to accommodate the heat. About 210 people lived in Pere and used canoes to traverse the waterways between homes.

The couple engaged workers to build a house for them and integrated themselves into village life. Participant observation was again the modus operandi by which Mead and Fortune gained information. Mead and Fortune also began using what Mead later called "event analysis," in which they organized their observations around village activities.

Mead set out to discover if spirits and ghosts populated the world of the seemingly carefree children, as they did the world of their parents. She collected about 35,000 drawings and found that the children concretized the objects they drew. None of the drawings reflected a humanizing of inanimate objects, such as drawing a moon with a human face. The huge number of drawings was needed, she wrote, because dealing with negative cases is a more difficult problem in fieldwork. Mead's research needed to prove that the Manus children did not display the animism of the adults; if their drawings had dealt with ghosts and spirits and given life to inanimate objects, not as many illustrations would have been required. Ultimately, as with her work in Samoa, Mead's research disproved a biologically based theory; the animism of the adults was culturally learned, not based on childlike mentality.

Although Fortune had received a fellowship at Columbia University, his and Mead's return trip to New York was delayed. While Mead enjoyed a wonderful six weeks on a plantation in New Guinea, Fortune made a side trip to take photographs of the Dobuans for his first anthropological book. In the summer of 1929 Fortune and Mead arrived in the United States but surgery postponed her return to New York. In San Francisco, Mead sought out a physician referred by her mother to operate on her sinuses with the hope of curing her persistent muscular discomfort. The doctor was obsessed with his theory about the relationship between sinuses and muscle pain and convinced Mead to allow him to operate. The surgery went awry and Mead almost died.

COMING HOME TO DEPRESSION AND FAME

Margaret and Reo at last arrived to New York in September 1929, a month before the fall of the stock market and the bank closures that signaled the start of the Great Depression. Margaret, who had followed her father's advice in being conservative with her money, was appalled to find that many of her friends, mostly academics with small salaries, had put all their savings into risky stocks. Benedict tried to convince Margaret to do so, but Mead kept the royalties earned by *Coming of Age in Samoa* in the small Doylestown, Pennsylvania, bank. It was a wise move and provided money for future trips in the field, since not only were staff salaries at the American Museum of Natural History cut, but Reo had deposited his money in a bank that failed. Margaret's father, who predicted wars based on the price of gold, warned her to expect a major war within ten years.

Mead's seventy-five page dissertation, "An Inquiry into the Question of Cultural Stability in Polynesia," earned her a 1929 doctorate in anthropology, but her future was shaped by the 1928 publication of *Coming of Age in Samoa*. Margaret had heard her book was successful, but she had no idea until she returned to New York in early autumn 1929 that sales had raced beyond everyone's expectations.

Coming of Age in Samoa was perfectly timed and content-rich for the times. Americans were intrigued by a book that described with exuberance a little-known culture in far-off Oceania. Mead's writing, too, for an audience of general readers in the mid-1920s, was slightly suggestive and titillating, as, for example, her discussion of the Samoan attitude toward homosexuality as "play." Homosexuality was, Mead wrote, looked on neither negatively nor positively because of a "general preoccupation with sex, the attitude that minor sex activities, suggestive dancing, stimulating salacious conversation, salacious songs and definitely motivated tussling are all acceptable and attractive diversions" (1961a: 148). Combined with insights that would help Americans understand the adolescent—that strange new breed that was suddenly appearing on the scene as an entity in it own right—it is no wonder the book sold to lay persons and social scientists alike.

In the introduction to *Coming of Age in Samoa*, Mead wrote that she went to Samoa to discover if the problems that troubled American adolescents were the result of their culture or were inherent in all adolescents during that time in their lives. If she found a culture in which young people passed without problems from childhood to adulthood, then the stormy, stress-filled years of American young women were culturally induced, not innate.

In answering her questions, Mead pushed readers in the Western world to question whether their civilized way of life was superior to that of a so-called primitive society. Mead's work took on extra meaning because her book, which emphasized that culture, not biology, was primarily responsible for how people behave, negated long-held reasons for racism and altered the way people had been taught to believe. In supporting the validity of people who were different, the book challenged the view that heredity alone was responsible for cultural differences; it supported Boas's contention that an adolescent's culture impacts the young person's transition to an adult world. In the nurture versus nature debate, there was no doubt that Mead supported nurture.

While many, especially academics, have faulted Mead for appealing to the masses in her writing, she took anthropology from a little-known, esoteric area of the social sciences into public consciousness. In the process, the name *Margaret Mead* became recognized around the world.

WORKING AT HOME

Mead and Fortune spent the next two years in the United States. During the first winter, 1929–1930, while Fortune finished *Sorcerers of Dobu*, Mead worked on her second book, *Growing Up in New Guinea*, which was published in 1930. Mead later said that the book's title should not have been so similar to that of her first book, *Coming of Age in Samoa*. People wrongly combined parts of the two titles and confused the books (Grinager 1999: 143).

The next summer, in 1930, the couple left for Mead's only field-work within the United States. The American Museum of Natural History asked Mead to undertake a brief study of Native American women. She initially felt slighted by the offer, since her previous field-work was more formidable, but the pot was sweetened when Benedict found funding for Fortune and husband and wife could work together. Benedict suggested Reo travel to Nebraska to investigate why no visions, prevalent in the folklore of most Indian nations, had been recorded in Omaha folklore. After analyzing the spirit world of the Dobu and the Manus, Reo seemed the perfect person to investigate the problem.

FIELDWORK WITH THE OMAHA

Mead described fieldwork with the Omaha as "a devastating experience" (1972: 206) for both her and Fortune. A combination of factors—the dry heat, the horrendous road trip during which Reo's driving terrified her, and the oppressive atmosphere of the reservation—made the three months of fieldwork tedious and difficult. The Omaha had discarded their old ceremonies and had not substituted in their culture anything that Mead and Fortune found attractive or satisfying.

Other problems added to Mead's sense of forlornness. They had to work through interpreters, since learning the language in three months was an impossibility. Because Native Americans had been frequently interviewed for many years, the Omaha saw anthropologists as a source of money for which they would tell anything or nothing. Mead was also appalled by the circumstances of the Omaha, a depressed people whose spirits seemed broken by poor governmental policies by the United States toward them over the years.

Added to these difficulties was Fortune's feeling that he had been set up to fail. He was furious when he learned that authentic ceremonial rituals were no longer practiced, that money was more important to the Omaha than the preservation of their past, and that many of the elder men thought revealing secrets would bring death. Mead wrote to Benedict that their work was discouraging.

Despite the problems, Fortune found that only men with a hereditary right to secret knowledge were believed when they claimed to have had a vision; the visions of others were discounted. Mead felt that Fortune did an excellent detective job in unraveling the reasons for lack of visions and never received the credit he deserved when *Omaha Secret Societies* was published in 1932.

The first major criticism of Mead's work derailed plans to return to New Guinea in the spring of 1931. A review of *Growing Up in New*

Guinea, written by a student of Bronislaw Malinowski, faulted Mead for her explanation of the Manus kinship system. Malinowski, a prominent anthropologist born in Poland, had immigrated to England to teach at the University of London. In 1922 he won high praise for *Argonauts of the Western Pacific* and was to the British school of anthropology what Boas was to the American. Mead believed that Malinowski had inspired his student's critical comments. For Mead to accept a negative review she believed unjustified was untenable and she felt compelled to remain in New York and write a technical monograph, *Kinship in the Admiralty Islands*, published in 1934, to refute the criticism.

For Mead, the depression was having minimal impact. The world was hopeful, during the summer heat of June 1931, that President Herbert Hoover's proposal for an international moratorium on war debts and reparations would cool down international monetary problems and avert a worldwide crisis. The worst of the depression was yet to come, but Mead and Fortune were on their way back to New Guinea by the end of that summer.

In September, when a deepening depression gripped the Western world, Margaret and Reo's foremost concerns involved finding porters to take their supplies—and Margaret—over the Torricelli Mountains, to the northern coastal range of New Guinea. Although Mead probably had yet to face actual and consistent violence, either verbal or physical, in her marriage, she realized life was smoother with Reo when they were away from New York, home to her but not to him. She anticipated fewer difficulties in their marriage on the trip to New Guinea, since in the field their personalities seemed to complement each other rather than clash.

Chapter 5

MIDCAREER LIFE CHANGES (1929–1939)

> A culture shapes the lives of those who live within it.
> —Mead, *An Anthropologist at Work* (1959)

From autumn 1931 until spring 1933, Mead and Fortune lived in three New Guinea villages, with peoples called the Mountain Arapesh, the Mundugumor, and the Tchambuli. Each provided different information about the societal roles of females and males. Mead's fieldwork resulted in a third book, *Sex and Temperament in Three Primitive Societies,* published in 1935—and a third husband.

HEALTH PROBLEMS

Mead, intellectually gifted, exceptionally active, never athletic, was only marginally robust and suffered many physical ills throughout her life. Of course, she put herself in situations that left her open to health problems, such as the recurring malaria that was carried by tropical mosquitoes and interrupted fieldwork with chills and fever. Bouts of neuritis and muscle pain began at college, continued throughout her life, and led to almost fatal surgery. A tipped uterus, which Mead was told prevented her conceiving, helped precipitate divorce with Luther, and a broken foot from an accident kept her on crutches for two months while married to him. She suffered in Manus from a second break with a resulting weak ankle that became progressively worse later in life when she suffered two additional breaks.

Mead's lack of stamina as well as her weak ankle made the trip through the inland of New Guinea difficult. She had to be carried on a hammock-type conveyance, laced in and covered with banana leaves to protect her from sun and rain. The trip made her feel seasick, she later wrote (Mead 1977: 103).

When Mead and Fortune reached the village of Alitoa, their porters refused to take them or their six months of supplies farther. They had no choice but to stay with the people they eventually called the Mountain Arapesh, a name they created from the native word for "human beings."

THE ARAPESH

Reo made numerous expeditions from Alitoa but Margaret's ankle forced virtual imprisonment within the small village and sent her into the only depression she admitted experiencing. Three months without mail and sporadic news via radio made the situation seem worse, and Fortune, reared to believe disobedience merited physical punishment, became angry easily and threatened to hit the houseboys. Reo's attitude only worsened if Margaret intervened. Mead envisioned herself as simply recording another culture and learning little. She felt as if her intellectual life were over, and presumably conversations with Fortune were no longer engaging or creative.

Mead described an Arapesh adult as being gentle and good-natured. A division of labor by gender existed, but both males and females cared for the children. Mead acknowledged that there were deviants in the culture who were less gentle and that villages sometimes clashed with each other, but she wrote, "Warfare is practically unknown among the Arapesh" (1963b: 23). Fortune disagreed and his article on the matter, "Arapesh Warfare," was published in 1939. Each was involved with different aspects of the culture and was reporting from a personal point of view, a fact that Mead later acknowledged, after her divorce from Fortune, when she wrote to commend him on his article.

Mead saw the Arapesh as a simple people whose creativity was exhausted by speaking their language, with its eleven genders and the plural of at least half the words irregular and impossible to guess. Most news among the Arapesh, Mead found, was rumor, shouted from mountaintop to mountaintop with a howl that reminded her of dogs baying at the moon. When Fortune was away on his first expedition, news was broadcast that a runner would soon arrive with a message telling of his death. When the runner arrived and presented Fortune's message to Margaret, the villagers began wailing, certain he had been attacked with a tomahawk to the shoulder and arm. The note was only a request that Margaret send Fortune some tea.

Mead soon found that for the Arapesh, "The whole adventure of living centered on making things grow—plants, pigs, and most of all, children" (1972: 214). A government agent had at one time distributed seeds and, while most native people would have been skeptical of using them, the Arapesh enthusiastically embraced growing and eating the vegetables. In a letter on February 12, 1932, Mead wrote that they enjoyed fresh vegetables most of the time and questioned, "Who would expect to meet a stark naked *man-o-bush*, very dignified in his shell necklace, walking in one's door with a banana leaf full of tomatoes?" (1977: 109).

In the same letter, Mead described the Arapesh as "ethnologically unobtrusive" (109). They considered Fortune and Mead the equivalent of a convenience store at which they could purchase items like salt and matches at any time and were willing to talk while the children played quietly with Mead. "They never go beyond sensation—the five senses, with sight and hearing only lightly exercised, and the brain never" (109).

Speaking at a 1978 conference in Los Angeles only months before her death, Mead used Arapesh intellectual skills to support her contention that culture was more responsible than biology for moving the Arapesh into modern life. When she initially studied the Arapesh, she said, they couldn't count and thinking made their heads ache. Yet in 1978 the Arapesh were succeeding in college and their country, now Papua New Guinea, was a new member of the United Nations. She concluded, "And their genes are just the same as they were twenty thousand years ago" (Grinager 1999: 251).

THE MUNDUGUMOR

After almost eight months with the Arapesh, Mead and Fortune decided to move on. They arbitrarily selected an area along a tributary of the Sepik River in the northwestern area of what is now Papua New Guinea. Kinakatem, one of six Mundugumor villages, had a rich culture, was easily accessible (important, given Mead and Fortune's previous difficulty with porters), had been little influenced by foreigners, was under minimal government control, and had not been appropriated by other anthropologists. Territoriality mattered in an era in which anthropologists were considered to "own" the area they were researching.

The Mundugumor (now known as the Biwat, for the river near which they live) were a culture in the midst of change. The Australians had recently forced them to abandon cannibalism, but to Mead they remained a warlike people. She found them "superficially agreeable, but . . . they go in for cannibalism, headhunting, infanticide, incest, avoidance and joking relationships, and biting lice in half with their teeth" (Mead 1977: 133). She described how young boys gleefully recalled eating human flesh but shuddered with nausea at the idea of eating a rat. Children were not valued in Mundugumor society and newborns were sometimes killed by throwing them, perhaps already strangled, into the river, although some were rescued from drowning, or at birth, by Mundugumors willing to adopt them. The Mundugumor word for *womb* was translated as "carrying basket" and a mother used a rough, stiff, semicircular basket suspended from her forehead to carry a baby as "preparation for an unloved life . . . begun" (Mead 1963b: 194). Nursing was done in a standing position with "none of the mother's dallying, sensuous pleasure in feeding her child that occurs among the Arapesh" (195).

Mead wrote in *Blackberry Winter* that the Mundugumor both "repelled and fascinated" (1972: 225) Fortune. She herself also seemed to have ambivalent feelings about them. She wrote that she detested their culture because they were an aggressive people who rejected their children (224). She presented a cheerier view in her letters, perhaps wanting to reassure family and friends, but she didn't take advantage of the opportunity to omit the positive comments when she compiled

Letters from the Field for 1977 publication. One of her letters, dated December 2, 1932, characterized the Mundugumor as "charming in many ways. . . . From these people we have wanted very little in the way of food and service and it has been very pleasant" (135–136). On February 1, 1933, she described a sacred flute she and Reo were given as a gift when they left the Mundugumor after three months with "friendlier adieus" (137) than they had received from any of the native peoples with whom they had stayed.

The sacred flute, considered the most important object made by the Mundugumor and representing power and prestige for its owner, was a special gift. The flutes are carved, usually from one piece of a hard brown wood, with the figure on top "swathed with shell, tusk, bone, beads, fur, hair, fibre, seeds, feathers and other extraneous material" (Fraser 1955: 18), and the elongated spike extending down from the top is also covered with lesser amounts of similar material.[1]

Fellow anthropologist Nancy McDowell, who made many trips to Papua New Guinea and, with Mead's blessing and initial assistance, analyzed and compiled Mead and Fortune's work in her 1991 book, *The Mundugumor*, wrote that the "society and culture were far more complex than anyone could begin to comprehend in three months" (7). Actually, as McDowell pointed out, Mead and Fortune collected most of their data in even less time, from October 4 to December 18, 1932 (6). Mead herself realized the material was thin, but offered several reasons for their early departure. Not only had the policies of the Australian government resulted in the abandonment of rituals, but unfavorable field conditions included mosquitoes that, like the Mundugumor, were warlike. Mosquitoes squeezed even into closed suitcases by the thousands. Nor did Mead perceive that she was gaining information related to male and female societal roles. With both the Mundugumor and the Arapesh, she thought that the cultural expectation was for adults to conform to one type; men and women did not have different behaviors. Even though time spent with the Mundugumor was brief, Mead considered their work very difficult, with little sense of satisfaction.

Annoyance with Fortune was probably an additional reason for leaving. He insisted that only he analyze the kinship system. When Mead discovered he had made an error in his work, she blamed him for sacrificing good scientific practice by too narrowly defining the area in which each of them worked.[2]

Even with so many problems constraining their work, McDowell credited Mead with an incredible feat of recording, organizing, and typing notes that enabled McDowell, fifty years later, to prepare them for publication. "If Mead had not been the organized and methodical fieldworker and excellent observer and chronicler that she was (almost all her notes were typed and labeled), this project would not have been possible" (McDowell 1991: 9). Fortune's notes, however, except for thirty-four pages Mead had typed, were mostly indecipherable.

Although McDowell's was the first ethnography (systematic study) of the Mundugumor, Mead's insights about their culture were described in *Sex and Temperament in Three Primitive Societies*. McDowell concluded that Mead "saw and recorded rich and vast amounts of material" (1991: 293) and in writing *Sex and Temperament* for the general public "condensed and oversimplified" the material as it "filtered through her theoretical lens. For example, her depiction of the Mundugumor is one of hostile, aggressive, and assertive people, but we know very well that there were meek and gentle Mundugumor as well. Many of the contradictory data—or data that did not fit precisely with this theme—while they do not appear in the published work, are labeled deviant in some way" (293–294). The idea of deviance is one that intrigued Mead and Benedict, even separated by half a world.

Mead and Fortune had been in the field over a year. Margaret was tired, ill with fever much of the time, and despondent because she did not yet see how her data would help her analyze the role of gender in a society. They decided to spend Christmas 1932 at Ambunti, a station maintained by the Australian government. On the way upriver they stopped to visit Gregory Bateson, who, on his third trip to the Sepik River area, was living with the Iatmul in the village of Kankanamun. His first words to the exhausted Margaret were, "You're tired," and he pulled out a chair for her. She felt that the words were the most endearing she had heard in many months (Mead 1972: 227).

GREGORY BATESON

Gregory Bateson was a brilliant English intellectual from a family of scholars. His father, William, or W. B., as his Cambridge students called him, was an eminent biologist and geneticist, an elitist scientist, and a nonconformist who "had no use for egalitarian trends" (Lipset 1977: 24).

W. B. married Beatrice Durham in June 1896, and Gregory, born in Grantchester, England, May 4, 1904, was the youngest of three boys. W. B. and Beatrice equipped their sons to follow in W. B.'s scientific footsteps. Gregory was even named in honor of Gregor Mendel, the man whose work with peas validated the theory of heredity, a slight irony since Mead, while not denying heredity, spent much of her life championing the role of culture.

Gregory received a BA in natural science and an MA in anthropology at Cambridge University. After a trip to the Galapagos Islands, he rejected natural science and, despite pressure from his father, accepted an offer made partly in jest by anthropologist A. C. Haddon to work in social anthropology for a year. The year after his father's 1926 death, to escape his mother's attempts to reincarnate her husband by manipulating her son's life, Gregory left to conduct fieldwork in New Guinea.

Margaret first heard Bateson's name when she was still married to Luther. Reo had written her that Haddon was kind to him but had gifted Gregory Bateson with his mosquito net. Reo ultimately had much greater cause to be jealous of the tall Brit.

OUT WITH THE OLD, RING IN THE NEW

Mead's 1932 holiday season at Ambunti was characterized by competing extremes among the Western group of seventeen men and two women. Bateson, Fortune, and Mead talked incessantly about issues related to anthropology. The rest of the group celebrated with so much drinking, smashing dishes, and tossing furniture out the door that Mead wheedled slices of bread and butter from the kitchen staff to tide her over until dinner was finally served.

Two days after Christmas, Fortune and Mead set off with Bateson in his large motorized canoe to search for a suitable field work site. They spent the first night of their trip with villagers who were expecting a raid. The raid never materialized but the possibility was frightening enough that the three took shifts sleeping and standing watch. Reo awoke to hear Gregory and Margaret talking; already they had developed a closeness that excluded him.

Despite life-transforming interactions with the two men with whom she was traveling, Mead was charmed by the beauty of the Sepik River. In a February 1, 1933, letter Mead described gliding in a small boat along *barets*. Similar to fens or canals, the water in them "is black, coal black, and shining with a dull lustre, and tasting like lily stems and sun-heated oil" (1977: 139).

THE TCHAMBULI

Mead and Fortune settled near Tchambuli Lake (also known as Chambri Lake), where the villages promised the ritually alive culture they sought. In addition, the Tchambuli were part of the broader Iatmul culture Bateson understood and whose language he spoke. Bateson decided to move closer to them and study another group living along the lake.

Mead, Fortune, and Bateson learned from each other. Bateson was dissatisfied with his calm, subdued approach, which netted him little information; however, his training in biology provided a broad theoretical base from which to compare and contrast. Mead's and Fortune's training had focused on the intense, systematic observation techniques Bateson lacked. The three anthropologists shared their styles of gathering and interpreting information and also genuinely liked each other.

Mead soon realized that the relationship had developed into a romantic triangle. To further complicate the situation, *Patterns of Culture*, the manuscript that arrived from Ruth Benedict, Mead's mentor, colleague, friend, and likely lover, cast a subtle light over the interactions of the three.

PATTERNS OF CULTURE

During 1927 fieldwork, Benedict had noticed substantial differences between the Native American cultures of the Southwest and the Plains. She had the sudden insight that, although one's personality develops within a culture, the culture itself takes on the patterns, or characteristics, of most individuals within that culture. She advanced the concept still further during the winter of 1927–1928 and presented a paper at the 1928 Congress of Americanists. Now Benedict shared with Mead, Fortune, and Bateson the manuscript that encapsulated her concept of culture as "personality writ large" (Mead 1973a: 206). The book described each culture emphasizing certain human traits, and the few people who did not fit the pattern of their culture because of innate or learned traits were deviants in their society, a concept Mead and Benedict had developed in past discussions over the years. Although the term *deviant* often has a negative meaning, to them the word simply meant straying from the norm, or the expected. Benedict did not see a limit to the number of possible temperaments. "No attempt to understand human cultures as limited by a given number of temperaments . . . ever pleased her" (Mead 1973a: 206).

PATTERNS OF TEMPERAMENT

Mead, Fortune, and Bateson devoured *Patterns of Culture* and discussed it thoroughly. It was relevant in a number of ways. Benedict had included information about Fortune's work with the Dobuans, and Bateson was looking at the related concept of ethos, which seeks to find a culture's distinguishing characteristic or tone.

As they discussed Benedict's book, the three anthropologists built on the concepts and began to ask themselves if types of temperament were neither male nor female but existed outside gender roles. Mead, Fortune, and Bateson developed a model of temperament type based on the points of a compass. Toward north were aggressive Mundugumor men and women, to the south, gentle and nurturing Arapesh men and women, facing west were Manus men and women, and facing east were

(Margaret hazarded a guess that turned out to be correct) possibly Balinese men and women.[3]

As they moved their discussions from the cultural level to the personal, Reo began to feel excluded. Gregory and Margaret saw themselves as nurturing; Reo as a northerner temperamentally fit the expectations of his native New Zealand society, although he also showed a tendency toward unchecked impulsivity.

Mead and Reo cabled Boas that they were returning home with new, potentially significant theoretical ideas. Although Mead did not directly use the points of the compass in *Sex and Temperament*, they influenced her writing and inspired her future field trip to Bali. Reo later repudiated their work and Gregory and Margaret did not publish, perhaps because their compass configuration was not supported by research, perhaps because by the end of World War II cultures were seen as too complex to be characterized with a single word or phrase; or perhaps because, with the theoretical basis of temperament resting on traits present at birth, its orientation was biological rather than Boasian, or cultural.[4]

MALE AND FEMALE ROLES IN A CULTURE

As Mead collected data on the Tchambuli, she realized that the dominant role women played in their culture provided the missing piece to her research puzzle. She fitted the pieces together in *Sex and Temperament in Three Primitive Societies*, in which Mead described both Arapesh men and women as gentle and nurturing, the way American women act; both Mundugumor men and women as aggressive and managerial, the way American men act; and the Tchambuli as reversing typically American expectations for men and women. Thus, she concluded, gender characteristics vary from culture to culture and are determined by the culture, not biology. "We are forced to conclude that human nature is almost unbelievably malleable" (Mead 1963b: 280).

In the preface to the 1950 edition of *Sex and Temperament* (1963b), Mead acknowledged the improbability of her finding "three tribes all conveniently within a hundred mile area" that allowed her to show gender behavior is molded by society. "This, many readers felt, was too much. It was too pretty." Mead responded politely but firmly to those who questioned her professional integrity by noting that the role of an anthropologist is to be open-minded about what one found. She also pointed out that the most minute happenstance would have sent her to a different village and changed entirely the resulting book. The selection of the three groups represents a sequence of more choice points in her life, in this case seemingly small decisions that provided the material for one of her best-known books. Mead herself used the term *serendipity* to describe the amazing series of circumstances.

Mead's conclusions may owe as much to psychosis as serendipity. "Bateson later said . . . 'All three of us together were pretty well psychotic'" (Howard 1984: 161). Richard Warms, anthropology professor at Southwest Texas State University and coauthor of *Anthropological Theory: An Introductory History* (McGee and Warms 1996), explains, "Basically, here is Mead sitting around reading a book written by her female lover, contemplating her relationship with two male lovers, one extremely rough and dominant and the other more gentle and sophisticated, and deciding that sex is culturally relative. It's hard to escape the conclusion that whatever might be true of the Arapesh, Mundugomor and Tchambuli, Mead's analysis owes as much or more to personal issues as it does to the characteristics of these people" (R. Warms: personal communication, February 7, 2002).

Regardless of Mead's motivation for her conclusions, what was radical about the book, Hilary Lapsley claims, was Mead's position that "men and women can be other than they are" (1999: 237) if their society permits their moving outside culturally dictated guidelines.

HOME, OF SORTS

Mead, Fortune, and Bateson arrived in Sydney in the spring of 1933. From there, Mead returned to the United States with the material for *Sex and Temperament*, and Bateson left by freighter for England with the material for *Naven*, published in 1936, in which he described Iatmul ritual.

Fortune and Mead were moving toward a divorce and Reo alone had no idea where he would go or what he would next do. Howard described him as seeing Bateson off, standing "with a pineapple in one hand and a pawpaw in the other. 'This,' Fortune said to the man who would succeed him as Mead's husband, 'is extremely symbolic'" (1984: 166). Reo was indeed left holding the fruit.

DIVORCE

Mead felt that marriage to men from a different culture was difficult. If culture is personality writ large, then personality may be culture writ small, and although Mead never publicly accused Fortune of physical abuse, she alluded to it when she noted in *Blackberry Winter* that he came from a culture in which "men beat women" (1972: 216) and wrote about his impulsive temperament. She confided to a friend years later that his knocking her down precipitated a miscarriage while in New Guinea, but she was prone to miscarriages and it is unknown the degree to which he was responsible. Given the triangular situation while with the Tchambuli, violence would not be surprising. Biographers have also described Fortune's paranoia, the difficulty he had not being the breadwinner, his "puritanical jealousy" (Bateson 1984: 155), moodiness, and outbursts.

The marriage survived while Fortune and Mead collaboratively produced quality work. He possessed a brilliant mind and his insights provided the impetus for them to develop and refine research techniques. Mead wrote that by the time of their second trip to the South Pacific they had developed innovative methods of collecting data. Although Fortune's anger and demands irritated Mead, his major error in insisting that only he deal with Mundugumor kinship, coupled with the excitement of work with Gregory Bateson, struck a final blow to the marriage. Again Mead sought a Mexican divorce and in 1935 was free to marry Gregory Bateson.

A REVERSE OF FORTUNE

Fortune seemed to have been more scathed by his marriage to Mead and their divorce than were Cressman or Bateson. In late 1934 or early 1935 he was suffering from fever, chills, and hallucinations caused by malaria when threatening tribesmen in New Guinea ambushed him for several weeks. This episode, combined with Mead's rejection, seemed to stall his creative life early in his career.

In 1937, Reo married Eileen Pope, the sweetheart he was trying to forget when he boarded the SS *Chitral* in 1926. After traveling and then living in Canada, they settled in England in 1947 and he taught at Cambridge. In the years until his 1979 death, Fortune kept silent publicly about personal displeasure with Margaret, although in private correspondence he snipped at her and his notes and copies of Mead's and Benedict's books "are studded with points of disagreement" (Lapsley 1999: 242).

THE SCHOOL OF CULTURE AND PERSONALITY

Mead spent much of the summer of 1934 wrestling with the concept of temperament and other issues related to human development at the multidisciplinary Hanover Conference held in New Hampshire. The conference was organized by Larry Frank, who subsequently played an important role in Mead's life.

The Hanover Conference led to a collaborative project between Mead and Benedict that produced *Cooperation and Competition Among Primitive Peoples* (1937), "an excellent, if inexplicably neglected book" (Lapsley 1999: 235), edited by Mead and contributed to by young anthropologists. It also provided the venue for formally introducing the anthropological school of culture and personality to the world of social science.

Mead, Benedict, and Sapir are considered the initiators of the school of culture and personality, which built on Boas's vision and evolved into the discipline of psychological anthropology.[5] In 1927 Sapir presented "The Unconscious Patterning of Behavior in Society," at a symposium on mental health. Published the next year, it is considered to mark the beginning of the school of culture and personality, but the deterioration of Sapir's personal relationships with both Mead and Benedict negatively impacted their work as a threesome.

Mead and Benedict, however, joined by others with a Boasian bent, continued to internalize and weigh information about the relationship between personality and culture and eventually psychological anthropology moved to the mainstream of American anthropology and flourished until the 1950s (R. Warms, personal communication, February 11, 2002). Although approaches evolved over the years, Philip Bock, emeritus professor of anthropology at the University of New Mexico, in *Rethinking Psychological Anthropology*, wrote, "Margaret Mead must be considered the major figure in the culture and personality school" (1999: 58).

MARRIAGE TO GREGORY BATESON

In February 1936, Margaret, with a trousseau of silk lingerie, set forth alone on another long ocean voyage across the Pacific. She and Gregory Bateson met in Java and flew to Singapore, where they were married on March 13, 1936. With his camera lenses wrapped in her lingerie, they sailed to Bali for an anticipated two years of fieldwork.

Bali was probably chosen by Margaret, and Gregory agreed to her plans. First, Mead saw Bali as allowing her to further explore the theory of temperament type. Second, she was offered support by the chair of the Committee for the Study of Dementia Praecox to study schizophrenia. Bali seemed an ideal location, since the Balinese "have culturally institutionalized dissociative and trance-like behavior, which in our culture is regarded as schizophrenic" (Jacknis 1988: 161). Third, Mead also wanted to continue studying the growth of children over a period of time, doable in Bali. And fourth, a former student, Jane Belo, showed Mead material on Bali, including films she had produced. The use of a new medium for collecting data was a motivator.

To Mead, Bali was an extremely congenial place for fieldwork. The Balinese culture was rich with tradition, a Western community offered friendship and support, and she was in love with a husband who was a competent professional and agreeable partner.

LIFE IN BALI

While a house was being built for them in Bajoeng Gede, an unsophisticated mountain community, Mead and Bateson gained an overview of all Bali offered. Mead was thrilled with the combination of Balinese and Western cultures. The Dutch had long been a presence in Bali and Mead and Bateson welcomed the Western influence. Roads made travel easy. An islandwide language, both written and spoken, rather than each village speaking its own language with no existing written counterpart, facilitated fieldwork. The use of money made a difference too. In prior cultures in which Mead worked, commerce was not tied to money; bartering was common, and if one did not wish to do something, the person refused. In Bali, money made business easier to conduct. Bali, however, was an island of contrasts. Although seemingly Westernized, Mead found that the Balinese had learned after several thousand years those foreign influences to embrace and those to ignore.

Mead and Gregory focused with great energy on the Balinese culture, rich with temples, art, music, and ritual, all of which the Western colony of artists, writers, and intellectuals introduced to them. Since travel was easy and feasts were staggered among the closely situated communities, Mead and Bateson were able to drive until they found palm-leaf streamers attached to gates or along the road, an indication a community was holding a feast or a theatrical performance. Performances and ceremonies as offerings to the gods, in short supply in New Guinea, were not only common in Bali but could also be ordered, as Mead and Bateson did when they wanted to film trance dances.

THE ANTHROPOLOGY OF VISUAL COMMUNICATION

The Mead-Bateson collaboration "pooled their respective complementary skills" (Pycior, Slack, and Abir-Am 1996: 277), with Margaret taking extensive notes and interpreting and synthesizing the information and Gregory focusing on film and photos to support Mead's notes. They worked feverishly far into the night, with each new opportunity challenging them to work with greater energy to refine a technique or to capture another element of the multidimensional culture.

The couple devised a technique that synchronized Bateson's camera work with Mead's notes by recording time. They were blessed with assistance from I. Madé Kaler, whom Mead described as a fantastic secretary who spoke five languages and had an extensive English vocabulary. He kept notes in Balinese and provided a cross-check on Mead's work. Bateson also used his own system to note relevant information; for example, whether the subject was aware of being photographed.

Instead of the 2,000 photos intended, Bateson shot 25,000 still photographs. He also used 22,000 feet of 16 mm film. "They had come to learn all they could about posture, gesture, painting, and the symbolism of play and dance; nothing around them could be dismissed as irrelevant" (Howard 1984: 195). To save money, they purchased processing equipment and eventually could develop up to 1,600 exposures in one evening.

Bateson and Mead considered the cameras alternative devices to record information. Mead analyzed Bateson's photographs to illustrate patterns they perceived, and the couple were later criticized that they used the camera to support preconceived theories. Although obviously their selection of subjects to film was subjective, Bateson and Mead were adamant that the events were not directed by them, although some subjects were posed and sometimes Mead asked children to act in a certain way. Mead and Bateson felt that they filmed so much that the villagers became unconscious of the camera's intrusion into their lives.

Their work made revolutionary use of the camera but did not make a dramatic impact on methods of conducting fieldwork (R. Warms, personal communication, February 7, 2002). So little attention was paid, Mead herself wrote, that when the American Anthropological Association held a 1971 visual communication symposium, their 1935 work was shown as a model of what could be done. Mead blamed anthropologists for being "uninterested in improving upon the pencil as a recorder of anecdotes" (Mead 1973b: 12) and they "selfishly sacrificed a research tool of immense potential to maintain an orthodoxy of words" (MacDougall 1978: 418).

There are two major reasons for the limited impact of their work on Bali. First, World War II intervened to draw their attention and time to more pressing demands. Second, since neither Mead nor Bateson was a full-time professor at a major university, they did not have the opportunity to disseminate information about how to analyze and bring order to massive amounts of film. In 1967, when Mead asked Sol Worth to share his photographs of the Navajo with a class, he simply presented them. The next morning she quietly showed him how to find patterns among the wealth of material that had overwhelmed him for the past year. This type instruction would have been multiplied many times over had Mead regularly taught and mentored advanced anthropology students. Mead wrote to Benedict that she was concerned her methods and techniques would be lost because she lacked university students as protégés.

RETURN TO NEW GUINEA

Although Mead and Bateson planned to return home after two years in Bali, they realized that the value of work in anthropology lies in comparing cultures. Returning to the Sepik region of New Guinea in March 1938 provided the contrasting culture needed to show how each dealt with a range of behavior, like feeding an infant. After approximately six months in New Guinea they went back to Bali for six weeks as a favor to Jane Belo and while there documented the growth of children Gregory had previously photographed.[6]

In Europe in the summer of 1938 Adolf Hitler had announced the beginning of Germany's march into the future when he took possession of the Sudeten borderlands of Czechoslovakia. By the spring of 1939 most people realized Hitler's greed for land was not satisfied and believed a second world war was inevitable. Thankfully, Margaret and Gregory ignored his mother's advice. Mrs. Bateson, concerned about war in Europe and not realizing Japan's entry into the war would push much of the fighting during World War II to the other side of the world, counseled them to remain in the South Pacific.

Mead and Bateson returned to New York in the spring of 1939. Since Mead evaluated her knowledge about other societies in terms of usefulness to the United States, she wanted to apply concepts of anthropology and psychology to the war effort. Mead also hoped she was pregnant, although she was unsure whether to deliver in the United States or England. World War II intervened, however, to make staying in the United States obligatory.

Mead, as a child, with her mother, Emily, 1905. (© Bettmann/CORBIS)

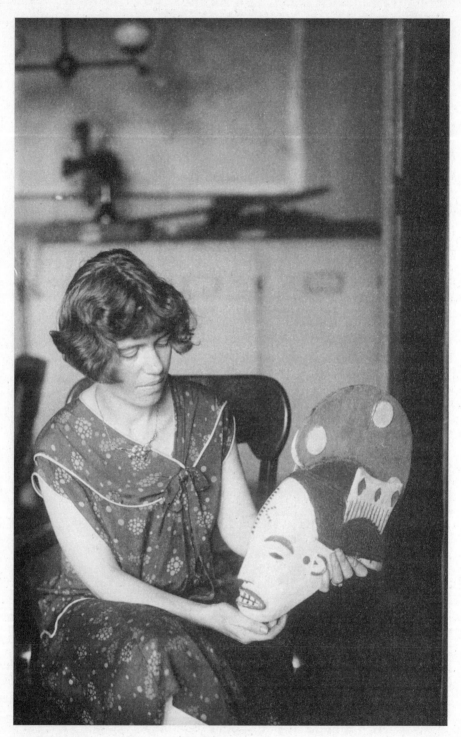

Mead holding mask. (© 2011 CORBIS)

Mead posing with artifacts she found in New Guinea, 1934. (© Bettmann/CORBIS)

Mead in Bali, 1957. (AP Photo/American Museum of Natural History)

Margaret Mead lecturing at the National Institute of Health, 1973.
(Courtesy National Library of Medicine)

Chapter 6

THE WAR THAT DIVIDED
THE WORLD (1939–1953)

> The trouble with life isn't that there is no answer, it's
> that there are so many answers.
>
> —Ruth Benedict, quoted in
> Mead, *An Anthropologist at Work* (1959)

On May 15, 1939, Margaret learned she was pregnant. She immediately took leave from the American Museum of Natural History and wrote at home while at risk for a miscarriage. Typically, Mead wanted as much control as possible and so decided how to organize the birth and baby's care and then work to make the process happen. She first selected Dr. Benjamin Spock as her pediatrician. Spock became a legend himself with the 1946 publication of *The Common Sense Book of Baby and Child Care,* a book that eventually sold more than 50 million copies to parents, who welcomed his message that they were competent judges of their child's well-being.

With his innovative approach to childcare, Spock readily agreed to four criteria—that he attend the birth and begin caring for the baby immediately; allow the birth to be filmed; agree to a wet nurse if Mead's milk were slow in coming in; and allow breastfeeding on demand. Spock then suggested an obstetrician he thought would be receptive to Mead's requests. Claude Heaton, also interested in Native American medicine, did have ideas compatible with Mead's, and so the team to deliver the baby was complete.

During the summer of 1939 Bateson and Mead worked to catalog the Balinese film and photos and Margaret contemplated what the child would be like. She felt strongly that the most important consideration was leaving the child free to develop in its own distinctive way.

German armies invaded Poland September 1, 1939, and Bateson, on advice from the British consulate, returned to England to help his native country with their war effort. He returned to the United States when his daughter was six weeks old.

MARY CATHERINE BATESON

Mary Catherine Bateson was born December 8, 1939, after her arrival was held up ten minutes while the photographer sent for a flashbulb. Her first name was in recognition of a distinguished Bateson aunt, her middle name, spelled with a C, in honor of those with the same name who had moved through Mead's life.

Margaret's breastfeeding, as well as her feeding on demand, rather than adhering to a rigid four-hour schedule, were not then common practices in America. In her memoirs about her parents, *With a Daughter's Eye* (1984), Mary Catherine Bateson pondered the strength her mother showed in insisting on caring for Cathy in ways that American doctors and nurses considered unorthodox and even unhealthy in 1939. In 1969, when Sevanne Margaret Kassarjian was born to Catherine and her husband, John Barkev Kassarjian, Bateson thought it "splendid" that Margaret was there as a grandmother to "robustly declare it was rubbish" (25) for mothers to fear suffocating the baby if they nursed in bed. Putting a baby alone in a separate room was the unnatural behavior, not nursing as one wanted and as women in other cultures around the world did.

Mead continued to advocate relaxed childcare and breastfeeding throughout her life. In the foreword to Dana Raphael's 1973 book *The Tender Gift: Breastfeeding*, Mead wrote, "The women's movement today embraces two groups, those who wish to permit women to be more fully maternal and fully feminine, and those who wish to use modern biological medical technologies to eradicate as many vestiges of our evolutionary past as possible" (5). Mead then stated she belonged to the first group.

For someone who considered herself "fully maternal and fully feminine," Mead relied on a number of other people to care for Cathy and did not hesitate to maneuver circumstances so she could fulfill professional responsibilities. For several years a live-in nanny and her teenage daughter helped. In July 1940, Gregory's teenage goddaughters, Philomena and Claudia Guillebaud, traveled to America to escape German bombs. They lived with the Batesons and helped care for Cathy until peace again came to Europe.

In 1940, American feeling against aggressively entering the war was so strong that both presidential candidates, Franklin D. Roosevelt and Wendell Willkie, stated a belief in aid only, not involvement. President Roosevelt maintained a public posture of keeping America neutral while still readying the country for war. In 1941 Japan seemed poised to conquer the Far East while the fascist forces of Hitler and Mussolini devastated British cities with endless bombing raids, raced through the Balkans, and stormed into Russia. In the United States, defense production increased, a draft law went into operation, and aid in the form of guns and older destroyers was offered to Great Britain, the only country that stood in the way of Hitler's conquest of Europe. Even though "the United States found itself in a virtual state of undeclared war with Germany," American public opinion could not bring itself to accept the entry of the United States into war. December arrived with "the country . . . still sharply divided emotionally" (Allen 1952: 162).

As 1941 drew to its end, Mead and Bateson had a stable home situation with Cathy, but the likelihood the United States would enter the ever widening global conflict made their professional futures, like those of many anthropologists, unclear. With fieldwork not possible, anthropologists living in the District of Columbia–New York corridor met to pursue ways behavioral scientists could apply their skills to the war effort. The Committee on National Morale, composed of about fifty intellectuals, including Mead, Bateson, and Larry Frank, was one such group.

Mead had been impressed by Larry Frank at a 1934 party when he first told her about his plans for the interdisciplinary Hanover Conference. Their ideas and interests were so similar and overlapping that Mead, Bateson, and Frank became close colleagues and friends.

WORLD WAR II

The United States officially entered World War II on Cathy's second birthday, December 8, 1941, the day after the Japanese bombed Pearl Harbor. The next spring the family moved in with Larry and Mary Frank, an arrangement then known as "for the duration" —that is, until the end of the war. The arrangement, however, lasted fifteen years. The Franks actually had two homes they shared with the Batesons, a house on Perry Street in Greenwich Village, and Cloverly, a summer home in New Hampshire that served as a weekend gathering place for social scientist friends. Mary Catherine Bateson wrote that she didn't realize what an important group of people passed through Cloverly until she recognized their names in her college textbooks (1984: 47).

Larry Frank had been widowed twice. His third wife, Mary, was a young, warm mother who willingly cared for Cathy in addition to her own young son, Colin, sixteen months younger than Cathy, and five children from Frank's first two marriages. Mead embraced this situation. As a social scientist, she knew the benefits of large extended families in other cultures, and the arrangement helped her balance family needs with a full professional schedule.

WORLD HUNGER AND FOOD SHORTAGE

Along with almost every US citizen, including their colleagues in the social sciences, Mead and Bateson contributed to the war effort during World War II. In 1941, Mead became executive director of the Committee on Food Habits of the National Research Council. She commuted to Washington DC, during the week and returned home on weekends.

Foods like sugar, meat, and butter were in short supply during the war and Mead and Kurt Lewin, a psychologist at the University of Iowa, directed experiments to study how food habits are formed, whether they can be changed, and how nutrition can be improved. Mead supported food being shared with other countries but realized it had to be acceptable in their cultures as well as palatable; for example, would people for whom rice is a substantial part of their diet use white flour? She traveled around the country to gather information and collect data to present at the committee's meetings two days a month. During her travels Mead's honest and direct insights garnered her many radio and newspaper interviews.

Mead seldom dropped ideas or people once they entered her life, and she continued her interest in nutrition and food production after the war. In a 1970 pamphlet published by the Scientists' Institute for Public Information, she wrote, "It is true that the principal nutritional diseases in the United States, as a whole, are the diseases of affluence—the results of too much and too plentiful diets—and not the diseases of poverty" (1970b: 4). She went on to stress that, while people had to be fed, the environment had to be protected. "When the hopes of feeding even more millions of people are tied to a worldwide disruption of the environment comparable to that which is threatening the more advanced countries with disaster, it is important to recognize the full complexity of the problem" (4).

ONE LANGUAGE, TWO CULTURES

Cultural issues had arisen between the United States and Great Britain and Mead was sent to Great Britain in 1943 to investigate. Even though the allies shared a language, which she later wrote was "theoretically mutually intelligible," Mead decided that in cultures related by language and tradition, "language confuses rather than clarifies" (Mead and Métraux 1953: 403); for example, the British perceived the world as one to which people adapt while Americans saw it as "a vast malleable space on which one builds what one wishes, from blueprints one has drawn, and when dissatisfied simply tears the structure down and starts anew" (404).

With a large number of American soldiers stationed there, Mead's official task while in Great Britain was to look at cross-cultural misunderstandings between men and women. Mead decided relationships between a British man and an American woman resulted in their continually arguing over who should make decisions, but in the reverse situation, neither the American man nor the British woman wanted to decide, even in matters so simple as whether to see a movie. In romantic situations, American males expected the female to determine the limits of a sexual encounter, but British females thought the decision the male's role.

Mead visited Cathy's godmother in London and speaking engagements gave her a chance to see England and Scotland. She found that many of what she considered Gregory's unique ways were in fact cultural.

STUDYING CULTURE AT A DISTANCE

In the summer of 1942 Mead wrote *And Keep Your Powder Dry*, her first book dealing entirely with her own country. The title referred to an admonishment, attributed to several figures in history, that directed soldiers to trust in God and keep their gunpowder dry, lest they be ill prepared to shoot. "To win," Mead wrote in referring to World War II, "we must take accurate inventory—not only of our copper and aluminum, of the number of skilled mechanics and potential fliers with good eyesight—but of our American character" (26). She spent only twenty-one days writing the book, and some wording suggests the speed with which she worked. "We are our culture" (21) and "Freedom's battles must be fought by freedom's own children" (26) have a ring of banality rather than insight.

Many sections, however, still hold interest for readers of the twenty-first century. Mead discussed the American attitude toward aggression and how this attitude impacts the ability of Americans to be successful as soldiers. To understand the conflict caused in young people by the mixed messages they receive about aggression, she suggested that readers study what adults tell children on the playground. " 'Jimmy! Look out, he's just a little baby, don't hit him.' 'Well, hit him back if he hits you. Don't stand there like a sissy and take it'" (141). Defeat at Pearl Harbor, Mead said, was not what forced Americans into World War II. No, she theorized with words that still resonate, it was that Americans carried a chip on their collective shoulders for years, but had been unwilling to engage in war until an aggressor knocked the chip off.

Mead acknowledged the Council of Intercultural Relations in her book, which became the prototype for studying national character as well as "culture at a distance."

INTERCULTURAL STUDIES

Mead, Bateson, and Benedict were members of the Council of Intercultural Relations, one of the small groups that met when the war imposed restrictions on travel, eliminating the opportunity for large conferences. Other members included Geoffrey Gorer and Alfred and Rhoda Métraux. After her divorce, Rhoda figured prominently in Mead's personal and professional life.

In 1935, Mead had met Gorer, an expatriate from Great Britain who had studied at Cambridge and whose interest in other cultures was fostered by study at the Sorbonne in France and the University of Berlin. A trip to West Africa in 1934 resulted in a successful book, *Africa Dances*, and Gorer gravitated toward anthropology as an adjunct to his interest in psychology. Gorer took courses in behaviorism at Yale but was never credentialed as an anthropologist. *Africa Dances* demonstrated his ability to detect patterns and caught the attention of Mead and Benedict, who encouraged and mentored him. He worked in the Office of War Information until 1943, when he left to work for the British embassy and recommended Benedict for the job. In 1941 Gorer had produced a short monograph, *Japanese Character Structure and Propaganda*, and Benedict continued the work of analyzing Japanese culture.

The Council of Intercultural Relations evolved into the nonprofit Institute for Intercultural Studies (IIS), officially founded in 1944 with Benedict and Mead as its directors. Its goal was to provide financial assistance to anthropologists seeking a cultural approach to international problems. Royalties, grants, and donations by a number of benefactors supported IIS work, with Mead herself contributing from her writing and speaking engagements, including the $50,000 advance she received for *Letters from the Field*. The IIS still exists and present commitments adapt Mead's philosophy to changing needs (http://www.mead2001.org).

BATESON'S WAR WORK

Mead's work during the war focused on the positive, but Gregory Bateson's work was so depressing that he considered suicide, although by a convoluted plan that involved parachuting into Japanese territory. He first worked in New York, teaching a course at Columbia University on what was then called pidgin English, to help troops going to the Pacific, and he later worked for the Office of Strategic Services (OSS, precursor to the CIA). In 1944 the OSS posted him to the South Pacific as part of America's psychological warfare program. His time spent in Burma, India, China, and Ceylon was depressing and discouraging. A sense of negativity permeated his assignments and he moved often in designing and implementing various propaganda plans. One job was operating a radio station with the goal of undermining Japanese morale. He was also dismayed by the realization that the desperate state of Indian agriculture in the Calcutta area, with consequent terrible famines, was primarily the fault of the British empire.

In later years when Gregory sought American citizenship, he was questioned about why, as a British citizen, he worked in the intelligence service of a foreign government—which, of course, was that of the United States.

IMPACT OF THE ATOMIC BOMB
AND ANTHROPOLOGY

Allied troops marched into Berlin on April 30, 1945, the same day Hitler committed suicide to effectively end the war in Europe, but the United States fought on against the Japanese in the Pacific.

Mead was horrified when the atomic bomb devastated Hiroshima on August 6, 1945, and then Nagasaki on August 9. Feeling the world had forever changed, she wrote in *Blackberry Winter* that she tore up every page of a book she was presently completing (1972: 296). Actually, she did not destroy the entire book; about 200 pages of various chapter drafts from *Learning to Live in One World*, dated July 9, 1945, and a second book Mead began after Japan's surrender, exist with her papers at the Library of Congress.[1] Mead was correct, however—the world had indeed changed.

The effect anthropologists had on the war effort is difficult to determine. Many of their reports were viewed negatively because a pervasive feeling existed among military strategists that social scientists were too impractical and idealistic. Although Gorer and Benedict and their colleagues thought the Japanese emperor should remain on the throne to ease Japan's transition to the postwar period, the degree to which their input entered into this decision is not known.

In the draft to *Blackberry Winter*, Mead cynically wrote lines that were cut from the final version: "the social scientists . . . took their marbles and went home" (as cited in Lapsley 1999: 293). Her pessimistic tone was probably caused in part by national and personal events in the years that immediately followed.

RESEARCH ON CONTEMPORARY CULTURES

In 1944, just before the end of the war, Benedict's connections in Washington, DC, led to a $100,000 grant from the Office of Naval Research for the study of culture at a distance, which later functioned under the name Research on Contemporary Cultures. The goal was to interview people who had immigrated from a foreign culture and develop a composite picture of a culture. The project turned into a huge effort, with 120 people studying seven cultures. The seed money was supplemented with additional funding and many of the participants worked for minimal pay, but the project's results were ultimately disappointing.

In 1946 Benedict's book *The Chrysanthemum and the Sword* was published. Begun during World War II, the book presents a picture of the Japanese that shows how they are different from Americans. The book was popular in both countries and, as one of the first studies of the Japanese national character, helped trigger what eventually amounted to "700 titles . . . published on the theme of Japanese identity in the thirty years after 1946" (Stewart 1992: 15).

Although the book was a sales success and well reviewed, it has also been faulted. Finding patterns that then lead to overgeneralizations about a complex culture seems itself to be a recurring pattern in the work of Mead, Benedict, and others in the school of culture and personality. Michael Salovesh, president of the Association of Senior Anthropologists (2000–2002), considers the book "fascinating, enlightening, and . . . not dependable. What I mean by that is that Benedict's book made sense out of what I saw around me in ways I wouldn't have figured out by myself: that was the enlightenment part. But as I came to know more and more Japanese people, I began to think that every new acquaintance was another anomaly if considered from Benedict's viewpoint" (M. Salovesh, personal communication, December 14, 2001).

Benedict, of course, had no direct contact with Japan, but her astute ability to perceive and her facile use of language served her well in writing *The Chrysanthemum and the Sword*. John McCreery, an anthropologist who lives and works in Japan, says, "This is a book, written in wartime, based on secondary sources and interviews with Japanese internees, including American citizens, by someone who never visited Japan. That it succeeds as well as it does is a tribute to Benedict's insight and skill as a writer" (J. McCreery, personal communication, December 13, 2001).

Despite the book's overgeneralizations about the Japanese, its success led to other books on national character that were not tributes to their authors' insights and writing skills. One of these was *The People of Great Russia*, written by Geoffrey Gorer and psychologist John Rickman and published in 1950. It was intended to help Americans understand Russian culture during the Cold War but turned into an embarrassment. Gorer reasoned that the Russian habit of wrapping babies tightly and restricting movement most hours of the day was responsible for their growing up to be suspicious and despotic. This "swaddling hypothesis" was such a simplistic view of a complex culture that it seemed ridiculous. Mead did herself no favors when she consistently defended Gorer, although she did not emphasize the swaddling hypothesis in her book *Soviet Attitudes Toward Authority* the following year, an omission on which she was complimented by several reviewers. Reviewers did, however, note other improbable theories.

The Study of Culture at a Distance (1953), edited by Mead and Rhoda Métraux, who was becoming increasingly more valuable as Mead's colleague and friend, was dedicated to Benedict. The book was intended as a manual for the Research on Contemporary Cultures group and its purpose was to provide the reader access to "methods that have been developed during the last decade for analyzing the cultural regularities in the characters of individuals who are members of societies which are inaccessible to direct observation" (3). Mead went on to say the changes in societies were now "so rapid and so revolutionary" (a word that in this context has multiple meanings) that anthropologists need methods for "reconstructing the cultures of a quarter of a century or even ten years ago" (3).

Despite laudable goals, the book was filled with verbose language; for example, in introducing the reader to what Métraux terms "resonance in imagery," in the chapter by that name, she wrote, "Studies of resonance in imagery are studies of imagery in different modalities" (344). Many pages contain intrusive footnotes that would have been better incorporated into the text. Even friend and colleague Cora Du Bois, in a 1954 review for *The Annals of the American Academy of Political and Social Sciences*, noted that "this collection is somewhat incoherent, but it contains charming, penetrating, and provocative vignettes" (176), although Du Bois concluded the writers had "contributed importantly to sensitivities and techniques in cross-cultural studies" (177). Mead herself wrote only sections, but as coeditor she was responsible for the book's content, and she accepted pretentious and hasty imprecise verbiage rather than the clear and stylish prose she championed earlier in her career.

Similar books on national character marked the end of the heyday of the school of culture and personality. Hilary Lapsley considers oversimplification of cultures by Mead, Benedict, and others in the school of culture and personality a result of the process they used, an "almost inevitable hazard of a search for unifying themes of a culture" (1999: 237). The problem of sweeping generalizations resulted in the school of culture and personality being swept away and moved anthropology during the 1960s in new directions.

DIVORCE FROM BATESON

In 1947 Gregory Bateson was a visiting professor at Harvard University. After, he lived for a while on Staten Island, New York, in the Richmond Borough, before permanently forcing Margaret to accept the designation of single mother by his 1949 move to California. Eventually, in 1950, he told Mead bluntly in a phone call that he wanted a divorce. Mead, concerned about a divorce's impact on their eleven-year-old daughter, flew to California while Cathy was visiting Gregory. After grilling steaks for a picnic, they explained their intention to divorce to their daughter. Catherine Bateson remembers asking about the possibility of a remarriage and needing to be assured again and again that they were not angry with each other.

In her memoirs, Catherine notes that her mother "grieved in secret" (1984: 58). Biographer Jane Howard wrote that Mead, after relaxing with friends over a few drinks, would sometimes become teary at having lost Gregory (1984: 313). Although Margaret insisted they had compatible temperaments, Catherine Bateson saw their contrasts in temperament more than the similarities. Gregory, a reflective, thoughtful person, essentially was detail-oriented and thought like a scientist. Margaret, on the other hand, had an appetite for recording details and minutiae but then sought the global view. Both thoughts and words moved rapidly from Mead's mind to her mouth. In 1980 Sey Chassler, the editor-in-chief of *Redbook* magazine, wrote in the preface to *Aspects of the Present* that Margaret "tossed out ideas at a rapid rate, but occasionally the rush of her thoughts and the mass of her information would tangle" (Mead and Métraux 1980: 5). Gregory also seemed to chafe more than either Reo or Luther about Margaret's urge to manage a situation.

Bateson merited status among many academics and became a cultural icon among younger social scientists, but he garnered little attention from a general public who simply could not relate to him and his ideas either through his writing or speaking engagements. In the introduction to *About Bateson*, a 1977 collection of essays attempting to explain the genius of Bateson, John Brockman compared speeches made by Bateson to two different groups during 1973. The first was a select group of his peers, "intellectuals, philosophers, psychologists, and scientists" (3), who were stimulated and invigorated by Bateson's talk. Several months later, Brockman, anticipating the excitement generated at the previous conference, found that Bateson had indeed been honest when he told Brockman that very few people understood the ideas he talked about. In this presentation to the general public, Brockman wrote, Bateson slowly worked his way "through his endless repertoire of concepts and ideas. He talks about metaphor versus sacrament, schismogenesis, metaphysics, explanatory principles, heuristic versus fundamental ideas, the value of deduction, steady state society, metapropositions, deuterolearning, cybernetic explanation, idea as difference, logical categories of learning, mental determinism, end linkage, and on and on" (7). Paying $100 to attend did not deter many in the audience from leaving. For his part, Bateson felt the problem was theirs if they could not or would not grasp his ideas.

Many who knew him found Bateson's avant-garde and freewheeling approach to life irresistible. Brockman wrote that Bateson's "child-like curiosity, his intellectual vigor and strength compel him to continue exploring new ground" (6). Those characteristics first drew Mead to him, made theirs a successful personal and professional union for over ten years, and eventually resulted in his taking the initiative to leave their marriage. He was the only one of her husbands to do so.

DEATH OF RUTH BENEDICT

Soon after losing Gregory, Margaret lost Ruth Benedict on September 17, 1948, at the age of sixty-one from a coronary thrombosis. Ruth had spent the summer teaching and traveling in Europe and was rushed to the hospital several days after returning home.[2] Mead stayed at her bedside the last five days of her life.

Benedict's *Patterns of Culture* was lauded as changing the definition of culture for many Americans from "not just the 'higher' arts but as a people's whole way of life" (MacClancy and McDonaugh 1996: 18) and providing "a sense of how an understanding of culture could increase an understanding of life" (Mead 1949b: 460). Benedict was respected among her peers in anthropology and in 1947 served as president of the American Anthropological Association. In an era in which women were often denied prestigious positions, Columbia denied her promotion to a professorship for many years. The university awarded her the position only four months before her death.

RENEWING HERSELF

Mead's way of coping with personal issues was work, so she set to turning a series of lectures she had given in 1946 on the psychology of sex into the book *Male and Female*, published in 1949. *Male and Female* incorporates Mead's perceptions of gender in many cultures, with an emphasis on the American psyche.

Reviews were generally positive, although many women thought the book took a step back from Mead's view that gender roles are culturally determined. They had applauded this view and found it liberating. That *Male and Female* reflected the conservative tone of the United States in the late 1940s and early 1950s, with World War II having receded into the past and the Cold War looming ahead, likely contributed to readers' resentment. Mead blamed misunderstanding of both *Sex and Temperament* and *Male and Female* on the difficulty Americans have in sorting out that which is innate from that which is culturally determined, without acknowledging her responsibility as a writer. And Mead, almost twenty years older, with three spouses in her past and a single child to rear in her future, was not the same carefree young woman who wrote about trysting behind Samoan palm trees.

RETURN TO MANUS ISLAND

When Mead heard about the rapid changes that had taken place on Manus, the island she and Reo Fortune had visited in 1928–1929, she decided in 1953 to return. Mead's making the right decision at various choice points in her life continued. Entering Barnard College and keeping the name of Mead were choice points that framed her entire life. Choosing T'au for her first fieldwork and settling among the Arapesh, Mundugumor, and Tchambuli were similar choice decision points that produced books renowned as classics. Arbitrarily choosing Manus for fieldwork in 1928 was yet another. And a quarter of a century and a world war later, Manus was the ideal site to study how rapid change occurs in a culture, because, as an irreverent and probably envious colleague put it, "the whole goddamn US Army trooped through New Guinea in the war" (as cited in Howard 1984: 297). Even before the Americans turned Manus into a major staging area, the Japanese had preceded them. Rapid change was inevitable and Mead was in the ideal position to lead a group studying that change. The American Museum of Natural History and the Rockefeller Foundation provided funding.

Going alone to Samoa with limited supplies and luggage at age twenty-five was an adventure, but it was now over. The garrulous Mead wanted and needed an entourage of staff to help her prepare for the trip and to accompany her. After an extensive search, she found Ted Schwartz, a multitalented anthropologist eager to conduct fieldwork with her. When Mead met the nineteen-year-old woman who became Ted's wife prior to their leaving, she decided Lenora would be the perfect second companion.[3] Lenora had no background in anthropology and had never traveled, but she had personal qualities, like flexibility and self-confidence, that appealed to Mead. In the months prior to leaving, Mead instructed them, or arranged for their instruction, in test administration, observation of children, field photography, use of equipment, and the cultures of places they would visit on their way to New Guinea.

Ted Schwartz recalled feeling as if they were taking a family trip. Ted and Lenora settled in M'bunai, a village not too distant from the house in Pere where Mead had lived a quarter century before. Rather than homes on pilings over water, the people now lived back from the beach. These houses were symbolic of the profound changes in their lives. Mary Catherine Bateson wrote that her mother told her that if people "who have dressed in grass skirts and shells decide to borrow Western dress . . . they must also borrow soap and needles and thread, or cotton clothing will soon be turned to rags" (1984: 177). So it went, with each new item of Western culture the people adopted necessitating the adoption of yet more.

The process of Westernization was bumpy for the Manus people. After the Japanese and Americans left, in 1947 a religious cult galvanized the people and led them to destroy their property and renounce their way of living, with the promise that a cargo of wealth would be sent to them. When it didn't arrive, Paliau Maloat arose as leader and the people of Manus had, as Mead said in the resulting book, *New Lives for Old*, "traversed in the short space of twenty-five years a line of development which it took mankind many centuries to cover" (1956: 21).

A volcano erupted a week after their June arrival and had the potential to create a tidal wave, which never materialized. Mead immediately took charge: "So I have some 250 people on my hands," she wrote in a July 2, 1953, letter home. "Each day I send people to some nearby market and into the bush to buy sago and taro to supplement the food the people have brought" (1977: 244–245). Sago, a powdered or granulated starch made from the pith of the sago palm tree, and taro, an edible plant root, were widely used in meal preparation.

Mead was satisfied with the response of her young colleagues to the potentially dangerous situation and they settled down to collect data. Ted and Lenora visited Mead once a week to share information gained from recording field notes and administering tests; Mead praised the notetaking technique Lenora developed from Mead's system. Many motor, visual, and cognitive tests were administered to the people. In *Confronting the Margaret Mead Legacy*, Lenora Foerstel (née Schwartz), wrote that testing took place almost every day, with people, including babies, lined up to participate (Foerstel and Gilliam: 1992).

Other than the heat, which routinely was ninety-six degrees with no cooling breeze, Mead's primary problem was in using so much time chatting with old friends who wanted to recall incidents from the past. Yet her background provided the substance for fascinating descriptions of people like John Kilipak, who had been the thirteen-year-old chief who cooked for her and Reo during their previous stay. Ted Schwartz later wrote that a study of modern Manus without Mead's background "would have been like studying embryology from scrambled eggs" (as cited in Howard 1984: 303).

With her usual optimism, Mead primarily saw the positive aspects of change in Manus. In *New Lives for Old*, Mead explained how the

Manus people, used to hard physical labor, loved the American use of engines to make life easier. She wrote that Americans "had engines to cut down trees and engines to saw boards and engines to lift loads" (1956: 174). With these engines they "knocked down mountains, blasted channels, smoothed islands for airstrips, tore up miles of bush" (168). Mead saw the Westernization of Manus as progress because she did not view it from the perspective of the Manus people but only from a Western point of view.

Mead returned to New York as 1953 came to a close, but the Schwartzes stayed on for a year, primarily to complete additional testing, Mead directed them to include photographing villagers for a study involving somatotype, or body type in their testing program. James Tanner, a physical anthropologist, was interested in classifying humans and then determining if a relationship existed between personality and body type. Mead wanted to help Tanner, despite the research being more involved with the role of biology than environment. Mead's keen interest in photography probably also influenced her agreeing to the testing and instructing the Schwartzes to complete it after she left.

Because the anthropologists received permission from the colonial administrators, permission from the villagers was not required,[4] but thirty-nine years later Lenora (Schwartz) Foerstel vividly described the nervousness and embarrassment she, along with the women, felt when Mead insisted Lenora photograph the women of Manus nude (Foerstel and Gilliam 1992: 65–67). Jane Howard, in her 1984 biography of Mead, added that when Lenora became ill after the photo session, the Pere people told her it was divine retribution, and she tended to agree (306).

Although Tanner eventually directed his research toward nutrition and health, Mead and other colleagues, including Barbara Honeyman Heath Roll, continued the somatotype studies to investigate physique on return trips to Manus and, although adults were photographed in loincloths, saw nothing wrong with photographing children nude up to their teen years.[5]

Mead returned to Pere village for what she called "field visits" (1977: 267) in 1964 and 1965; Ted Schwartz visited her for Christmas there in 1973 and 1975. Her final illness prevented an anticipated return trip.

When Mary Catherine Bateson visited Pere in 1979 to dedicate a community center to her mother's memory, she found her mother's perception of the village's march into the future had been "too clear and optimistic for the reality and yet the reality is impressive" (1984: 193). She judged her mother, in her assessment of Pere village's transformation, to have been "both right and wrong" (193).

Emilie de Brigard, in reviewing a film about Mead's life for *American Anthropologist*, the journal of the American Anthropological Association, summarized the narrator's comments that Mead spent "the first half of her life trying to save the world's tribal cultures, and the second half trying to save the world from itself" (1983: 494). When Mead returned from Manus in December 1953, she had completed the last trip in which she did a major share of the research. Although she traveled a great deal during the next twenty-five years, these expeditions were undertaken in her quest to improve the world through a demanding schedule of speaking engagements, extensive writing for both the popular and academic press, and unrelenting enthusiasm for remaining in the public eye "to save the world from itself."

Chapter 7

MEAD, THE POLYMATH

A Scholar with a Worldwide Perspective (1953–1978)

> First, if one puts oneself in a position to be asked questions in a public forum, one must stand up to the questions that are asked, whatever they may be. . . My second comment is that the anthropologist's one special area of competence is the ability to think about a whole society and everything in it.
> —Mead, *Margaret Mead: Some Personal Views* (1979)

By the 1950s Mead was recognized as an authority in many fields. In a 1961 article in the *New Yorker* magazine, Mead was quoted as saying, "The whole world is my field. . . . It's all anthropology" (Sargeant: 32), a mantra she often verbalized and translated into action as she studied, analyzed, and commented on every possible subject. A joke circulated asking what Margaret Mead said to the all-knowing Delphic Oracle. "She said, 'Hello, isn't there something you'd like to know?'" (Howard 1984: 386).

She was "by far the most widely acclaimed figure in her profession" and "a tireless public evangelist for the social and behavioral sciences" the *New Yorker* article declared (31). Jeremy MacClancy, professor of anthropology at Oxford Brookes University in England, wrote in *Popularizing Anthropology*, "No one has been able to put the anthropological message across, to a comparable extent, to non-academic audiences" (MacClancy and McDonaug 1996: 19).

Mead gained much visibility—some would say notoriety—through an organized schedule of activities that included speaking, writing, and teaching, and she overlapped these activities in a way that the information from one was used to complement another. William Mitchell, a student and later colleague and friend of Mead, wrote that "speaking engagements for Mead were a form of fieldwork" (1996: 124). When she spoke, Mead took questions from the floor, often by distributing cards to the audience. She answered some questions immediately—directly, honestly, thoroughly, and sometimes shockingly—and collected those that time didn't permit answering. She read and considered all the questions and, by scaffolding new information, she built book chapters or articles. In turn, her writing generated yet more speaking engagements. It was a cyclical process that kept Mead and her views in the public eye.

SPEAKING

Mead began making presentations to her mother's numerous women's clubs as soon as she returned from Samoa in 1926. Publication of *Coming of Age in Samoa* sent her on speaking engagements far beyond the limited corridor between Philadelphia and New York. The war and Cathy's birth slowed her, but after Cathy was in her teens Mead felt freer to accept the many speaking engagements offered.

Mead loved public speaking and at the height of her career spoke to over 100 audiences a year. Howard reported her as once complaining she was exhausted. "If only I could give a lecture!" (as cited in Howard 1984: 375). Mead was not an actor because she played herself, but she did put on a performance by speaking with conviction, optimism, and self-confidence, and by "provoking others to think unconventional thoughts about conventional things" (Mitchell 1996: 125). The Reverend Roger L. Shinn wrote that Mead could give "a dazzling lecture" without referring to notes and generate ideas "faster than most people could hear them" (Shinn 1978: 304). As a March 21, 1969, article in *Time* magazine noted, "For all the familiarity of her views, she remains an original, with a capacity to shock and surprise" ("Margaret Mead Today: Mother to the World," 74).

Mead's appearance and manner resonated with audiences, to whom a renowned speaker with the appearance of Everywoman, and later Every-grandmother, was a pleasant surprise. Physically, she was never considered a beautiful woman, but glasses, commonsense clothes, and short hair held over a steaming tea kettle to encourage curls endeared her to the public. She started wearing slacks in 1968 when she was sixty-seven and quickly realized their virtues. Prior to her losing bout with cancer, she gained so much weight she had difficulty fitting into an airplane seat, but "Mead was most successful in her hands-on, face-to-face, public appearances" (Mitchell 1996: 126).

Mead also performed masterfully for radio and television hosts. She was witty, charming, and direct. "Anthropologically speaking, she was probably one of television's first talking chiefs" (Grinager 1999: 117). narguably, she filled the role of official US orator and spokesperson on a multitude of topics, just as had the Samoan *tulafales*, or talking chiefs who acted as official orators for the chiefs, described by Mead in *Coming of Age*.

WRITING

A complete bibliography would list about 1,500 entries, or an average of 150 books and articles every year of Mead's half-century career, a prodigious output. She promised a sequel to her autobiography, *Blackberry Winter*, but then decided against it, reasoning that the earlier years of life are the most interesting and life becomes routine as one ages. Robert Cassidy, who later wrote *Margaret Mead: A Voice for the Century* (1982), proposed collaborating with Mead on a book that covered her life after *Blackberry Winter*. She agreed but they were able to meet only once before her death.

Two of Mead's later books, although not among her best-known works, were collaborations with photographer Ken Heyman. *Family*, published in 1965, and *World Enough: Rethinking the Future*, published in 1975, were photo-essays that illustrated her sparse yet poignant writing style and ability to analyze information and create a unique interpretation.

In *Family*, the first section, "Mothers," began with the sentence, "A mother accepts her child before she knows who that child will be" (13). The second section, "Fathers," began, "Children grow toward their fathers" (45). The black-and-white photographs came from multiple locations around the world. Many of the pictures on the same topic were in direct counterpoint to each other; for example, photographs of mothers bathing a child or children showed both similarity and difference, illustrations that proved what Mead in the introduction referred to as the "many kinds of people in the world, whose lives are full of contrast and yet are comparable" (10). Mead, sensitive to those less economically endowed, also commented that many of the families represented are poor, because "it is prevailingly the poor of the world who gather on doorsteps, in parks, and on public beaches. They lack space indoors and have no gardens where their children can play safely under the trees. They lack walls to shut the stranger out of their lives" (11). The format of *World Enough* was the same as that for *Family*, but the content discussed technological change, a seemingly dry topic brought to life by Mead's narrative and Heyman's photographs.

Mead also wrote articles for all types of print publications, but her most consistent writing was for *Redbook*, a magazine for young women. With Rhoda Métraux, Mead wrote a column for sixteen years. In one article, when Admiral Hyman Rickover wrote that members of Parent-Teacher Associations (PTAs) are "an infernal nuisance and ought to stay home and take care of their husbands" (as cited in Mead 1979: 162), she admonished him by replying that the weakness of PTAs is that they did not sponsor a GTA, with G for "Grandparents."

While most of her replies were in-depth, her shortest answer was one word. Question: "Do you believe in God?" Answer: "Yes" (Mead 1979: 176).

Mead consciously wrote for a lay audience but could, of course, write in technical jargon. As wittily summarized in the *New Yorker* article, "In purely scientific monographs, she proved over and over again that she could write as technically and obscurely as anyone else when she felt like it" (Sargeant 1961: 31). Even in her professional writing, Mead often maneuvered around the inclusion of specialized vocabulary by obscuring it in attached endnotes, so her style when writing for scientific journals was generally also direct, lucid, and graphic, but not so personal for professionals as for the public. In

"The Role of the Individual in Samoan Culture," an article published in the *Journal of the Royal Anthropological Institute of Great Britain and Ireland*, Mead described the role of the titled head of a large household (*matai*): "A man's accession to a title means endless responsibility for ten or fifteen individuals in the household under his charge—responsibility to the village council for their care, guidance and peaceful behaviour; responsibilities in the affairs of the village" (1928: 485–486).

A *matai* speaks for himself in *Coming of Age in Samoa*: "Thirty-one people live in my household. For them I must plan, I must find them food and clothing, settle their disputes, arrange their marriages. There is no one in my whole family who dares to scold me or even to address me familiarly by my first name. It is hard to be so young and yet to be a chief" (as cited in Mead 1961: 36–37).

Mead wrote at the same rapid-fire speed with which she spoke, usually several thousand words before breakfast, a monstrous task by any standard and more impressive in a pre-cut-and-paste era. Gregory Bateson confirmed her claim and said he simply couldn't keep up with her physically since she put in a full day's work at the American Museum of Natural History after her morning writing (as cited in Howard 1984: 253).

TEACHING

Although she served as a guest instructor at a variety of universities, Mead regularly taught at Columbia University. She was a visiting professor of anthropology at the University of Cincinnati College of Medicine for twenty-one years because Mead and Dr. Maurice Levine, the director of the Department of Psychiatry, believed in the interdisciplinary exchange of ideas. She also lectured annually at the Menninger Foundation in Topeka, Kansas, and was on the board of trustees.

Mead taught the way she conducted fieldwork, by participant observation. In *Uncommon Lives* Patricia Grinager wrote that Mead encouraged students to absorb information the way she had absorbed the Manus culture:

The Manus lived on water. She's told about going there, dipping into the water with them, swimming around, looking and listening; playing and entering into their activities. Unobtrusively. A part and apart. When she came out of the water, she made notes and then thought through what her notes meant in terms of their culture, as well as her own education in anthropology. She read ethnographies and travelers' reports. She interacted with the Manus people on a day-to-day basis for months on end. She ate their food, held their babies, helped at childbirth, doled out aspirin and Band-Aids, and took pictures.

She lived in a see-through house in the middle of the village. It had no walls. She could observe the villagers from anywhere inside her house and they could look in on her from anywhere outside. After a while, she began to understand Manus culture from the same two perspectives provided by that air-conditioned house: from the inside looking out and from the outside looking in. (1999: 103)

Her courses were always popular and eventually over 10,000 students could claim they had Dr. Margaret Mead as a professor. When she taught a course at Yale, 600 nonanthropology majors signed up. Given the huge number of students eager to personally be privy to her insights, she did not grade work herself but relied on paid readers to grade the essay exams. She also believed everyone should receive an A or B, a philosophy not likely to diminish the number signing up.

She did grade the work of students in her advanced courses with exceptional care and shepherded them through Columbia's doctoral program. Biographer Jane Howard wrote that Mead advised Vincent Crapanzano to take a map with him to his oral defense of his dissertation. When he said everyone on his committee knew where Morocco is, Mead told him he could bide for time in answering a question he was unsure about by pointing to something on the map (Howard 1984: 328).

Mead said she got her stamina from her mother and she did not need to choose between work and pleasure because to her they were synonymous. In her seventies, she maintained a full schedule that might include four speaking engagements at four colleges in a two-day period. To support her writing, speaking, and teaching, Mead enjoyed the backing of two prestigious institutions, Columbia University and the American Museum of Natural History. Both provided helpers to carry out the minutiae involved in her work and the museum gave her an office.

THE STEPS TO FAME

Mead's attic office in the west tower of the American Museum of Natural History was crucial for carrying out her agenda. To reach her office, she had to take the elevator to its last stop and then walk along a dark hall with no windows and up two flights of stairs. From the very first day of work in 1926, Mead cherished this office because it seemed similar to the attic accommodations in the Mead family's many rental properties during her childhood. She insisted on retaining the tower office even when offered a more prestigious location and it remained her domain until her death over half a century later.

While remembrances of childhood attic rooms may have influenced her decision to remain at the museum her entire career, she saw elderly curators continuing in their jobs at the museum. The university system, she noted, practiced age discrimination while clearly the museum was more flexible about retaining older curators.

The museum, like universities, did practice gender discrimination. Mead, despite her bestselling books, honorary doctorates, and multiple awards, remained an assistant curator until she was promoted to associate curator in 1942 and then finally made curator of ethnology in 1964, thirty-eight years after she began work there. Admittedly, her not advancing in the museum hierarchy was partially because the museum assumed a role of benign acceptance of her fame and tolerated her speaking engagements. Mead herself said that the museum considered her a tumor but as long as she remained a tumor, she felt safe. As a cancer, she would be in danger of being removed.

THE PAPER CHASE

Mead was not one to collect mementos while on a trip except for select items to add to the museum's collection. She owned so few personal possessions that she could easily store them in her portion of a shared apartment. What Mead brought home from trips were notes. Aware of the number of anthropologists who never transcribed their notes, she determined early in her career always to write up her notes before undertaking new fieldwork, remarking that a ceremony observed but never written up was time wasted.[1] At her death, she bequeathed more than 500,000 items to the Library of Congress in Washington, DC. This is one of their largest collections donated by a single individual.

Mead used both paid assistants and volunteers to manage the office and keep track of the immense flow of paper. Although she sometimes hired trained secretaries, she preferred untrained volunteer anthropology majors who were more knowledgeable about the field. She had two rules for whoever worked in the office: all mail and other papers had to be dated upon arrival and a copy had to be made of papers leaving. The latter was a challenge in a pre-copier era, when making copies required black carbon paper sandwiched between letter-quality paper and sheets of stiff tissue paper.

Mead kept everything and used the nooks and crannies, and even a fireplace, for storage of her voluminous materials and then blamed her staff for not being able to locate items she wanted at a moment's notice. Patricia Grinager, whose road to earning a PhD began with volunteer work for Mead, described such an event in *Uncommon Lives*. Mead stopped Grinager and several other staff as they were leaving one afternoon to demand copies of certain interviews collected by Ruth Benedict, who had died five years before. The staff at last found them in an unmarked cardboard box high on the top shelf of a bookcase (1999: 19).

Mead's temper was legendary. Since she traveled a great deal, the office was calm during her absences, but the atmosphere quickly churned up when she was present. Although Mead didn't physically abuse anyone, Grinager noted that "the combustion level of her verbal invective could have set the place afire without a match" (17).

Grinager herself would stand her ground when she felt Mead's anger was misdirected. Once Mead became furious when she discovered that a locked wooden footlocker containing hand-painted slides had been set atop a hot radiator. Grinager was the closest person and suffered Mead's blast. Grinager responded with her own heated reply, saying that no one could call her stupid. Although the slides were indeed in danger of being ruined by the heat, the locker was painted silver and blended in with the radiator upon which it sat, and Grinager told Mead that the box needed to be labeled since there was "no way in hell any of the rest of us could guess what's inside a locked box" (20).

Grinager, Frances Macgregor, who worked with Mead on analyzing the Balinese photos that led to the book *Growth and Culture*, and the Reverend Austin Ford, an Episcopal priest and friend, agreed that Mead became more reasonable when people answered back. Many office workers were reluctant to answer her in kind, however, and sought other means for coping. Ellen Godwin, who worked for Mead in the 1950s, engaged Gotthard Booth as a psychiatrist. Booth told Godwin (as cited in Howard 1984: 260) that in his practice Margaret Mead was one of the problems some people brought up for discussion. One way or another, office workers coped or they quit; Grinager credited Mead's extended absences from the office as being partly responsible for staff stability.

THE VIEW FROM THE TOWER

Although she spoke out on numerous topics, Mead was criticized for lack of sustained activism in any particular cause; for example, women's rights, nuclear test bans, and the environment. Mead, however, was neither a demonstrator nor a supporter of single issues. She believed that demonstrations were divisive and preferred to seek compromise. Rather than focusing on only one problem or issue, she was a synthesizer and interpreter who analyzed and explained information from numerous disciplines. "Her most important contribution," wrote Cassidy in *Margaret Mead: A Voice for the Century*, "was her ability to assimilate information from a wide range of fields, process the facts, and somehow create a whole new viewpoint" (1982: 155). Her insights on the generation gap are a prime example.

Generation Gap

As babies born immediately after World War II reached their late teens, the conservative and quiet 1950s gave way to the tumultuous 1960s. The decade started with the election of the first Catholic president of the United States and moved quickly to the possibility of Russian missiles aimed at the United States from nearby Cuban bases. Nuclear war seemed such a real threat that many families considered building home bomb shelters. Events in the Far East soon captured center stage, with the escalating war in Vietnam continuing until the capture of Saigon in 1975, while at home Martin Luther King Jr. led the fight for equal rights for African Americans. Just as upsetting to many older Americans were the changes that pervaded every aspect of life. Chubby Checkers introduced rock music and Britain's Beatles soared in popularity; an effective birth control pill freed many women, married or unmarried, from the threat of unwanted pregnancies; "drugs" no longer referred to those prescribed by a doctor; and the hair of males was often longer than that of females, who turned from wearing demure dresses to tight torn jeans. Adults were horrified at daily newspaper and television accounts of young people's protests, which ranged from the war in Vietnam and civil rights for blacks to panty raids in college dormitories. America was truly in a state of foment and torment.

Mead may not have coined the term *generation gap*, but she popularized its use to refer to the difference in sense of history between those who were born and reared before World War II and those born after it. She later felt the term was a poor one and that "era gap" better represented the conflict that occurs when a culture is in a state of rapid flux, but by that time the catchy term *generation gap* was embedded in public consciousness.

Mead described three types of cultural states:

> Postfigurative: traditional cultures that change little from generation to generation so that younger people learn to replicate the past from their elders; for example, the Amish, who reject changes in their way of life.
>
> Cofigurative: competing cultures in which a dominating culture wins out over another and children and adults learn from peers; for example, immigrants learn from members of their age group and then meld into the culture of the country in which they now live.
>
> Prefigurative: a culture in which change occurs continuously and adults can learn from children, as in the general population of the United States. The young "are at home in this time," while "nowhere in the world are there elders who know what the children know" (Mead 1970a: 58–60).

Mead saw the greatest potential for conflict among the young and old in the latter two types. She did not see the young simply rebelling against old ways but rebelling because they had a different perception of the world and wanted changes. Mead believed that as rebellious youth became responsible adults and moved into decision-making roles, they would solve the issues they had protested. They would also discover that protesting was exciting, but that actual change was not readily or easily achieved.

Mead had long considered the postwar ramifications of rearing children and anticipated the generation gap. In an address at the Mid-century White House Conference on Children and Youth, December 6, 1950, excerpts of which were later published in the journal *Understanding the Child,* Mead talked about guiding children in a rapidly changing world in which they could not learn by following their elders. "The most that we can do," she said, is "to present to our children a provisional picture of humility and confidence, an expectation that they, inheriting our pre-vision, may in fact have vision enough to carry on their task of cherishing and protecting the lives of men and the life of the world" (Mead 1951a: 17).

Mead expanded and refined her insights and in the 1960s wrote and spoke widely on the generation gap. Her 1970 book *Culture and Commitment: A Study of the Generation Gap* revisited cultures she described in her other books without adding appreciably to the theory. Although over the years the term *generation gap* has become popularized and trivialized through marketing, the concept of cross-generational ideological conflict is still valid.

Women's Rights

One area in which Mead's personal and professional lives clashed was women's rights. She skillfully tried to navigate the waters of feminism and femininity, but her public and private selves seemed to disagree on the direction to take. Although Mead disliked being called a feminist, her career was paramount in her life. As Phyllis Grosskurth wrote in *Margaret Mead*, she "always posited something of a problem to the women's movement. She competed on her own terms in a man's world, but she maintained certain traditional values about women" (1988: 49).

The topic of family in a variety of cultures dominated Mead's professional life. In *Blackberry Winter* Mead wrote that she had a sudden insight while talking with a professional group with her young daughter on her lap. She realized that women who have children are likely to be less productive because they have a baby who smiles too much and being a mother is "so satisfying that it has taken some special circumstance—spinsterhood, barrenness, or widowhood—to let women give their whole minds to other work" (1972: 270).

Conversely, in personal life, the reality of motherhood seemed less than magical. When Patricia Grinager lost her job as an administrator at Columbia University, Mead railed at her for taking a vacation to visit family in California. Women put their families first and then don't finish their dissertations and publish, but she herself had not been stupid like that, Mead yelled, completely ruining Grinager's luncheon appetite (Grinager: 109).

Mead's daughter, Mary Catherine Bateson, did not resent her mother's professional commitments. As a child, she often roamed the halls of the American Museum of Natural History, even before opening time and after closing, and once Mead arranged a birthday party there to show Cathy and her friends how the dioramas were built (Bateson 1984: 75). Cathy also stayed with "Aunt Marie," as she called her mother's friend Marie Eichelberger. Her mother's sister Elizabeth often cared for her when she left school early, and, of course, she visited with her own friends when Mead was unavailable or out of town. Bateson was a mother solving her own childcare problems before she realized the "complex infrastructure" (Bateson 1984: 74) her mother's life required to assure arrangements were made for Cathy's care.

Freedom of Choice

Mead believed that people were entitled to make their own decisions in personal matters such as interracial marriage, hair and clothing styles, and adoption of children by single women. At a time when abortion was illegal but some states were liberalizing legislation to allow its limited practice, Mead was in favor of the repeal of all laws controlling abortion, although she personally considered it "too close to the edge of taking life" (1979: 100). She believed repealing anti-abortion laws would allow a focus on contraception and "the development of life-styles and personal relationships that are consistent with the idea of conceiving, bringing into life and caring for children, all of whom are desired and loved" (100).

She felt similarly about euthanasia and wrote in the journal *Christianity and Crisis*, "Quite clearly no Christian can vote for abortion or euthanasia as public policy for reducing the population or lessening the burden that the support of the weak places upon the strong. But the need for laws that permit individual interpretations of the beginning and end of life is manifestly very great" (1973c: 290).

Marriage

Mead's biographer, Robert Cassidy, called several of her proposals "ill-conceived, impractical, or politically unfeasible" (Cassidy 1982: 13). Her proposal for two types of marriage was too radical for the public to accept. Mead blamed the high divorce rate in the United States on youthful marriage without adequate preparation. She first proposed a public school course that would cover budgeting, childcare, and similar problems, an idea that caught on. Then she proposed two types of marriage: individual, in which the couple was legally married but agreed not to have children or incur financial obligations if they parted, and parental, in which they contracted to rear children but which could only be undertaken if the individual marriage were successful. The furor, with very few in favor, ranged from those who said living together was easier than an individual marriage to someone who suggested Mead's plan was similar to "legalized prostitution" (Mead and Métraux 1970: 175). Mead stepped back from her position but with a stern lecture about the pitfalls of ignoring her advice. In an article, later included in *A Way of Seeing*, a collection of Mead's contributions to *Redbook* magazine, she concluded, "If you want the experience of full-time companionship with someone you love—and this is what you should want, for it is the most satisfactory and fully responsible relationship—you had better get legally married, use contraceptives responsibly and risk divorce later. You are risking even more if you don't" (1970: 183).

Some related proposals similarly did not generate support. Mead continued to see the benefits of matching temperaments and said she picked her friends by temperament. Picking children by temperament was a different matter. Mead suggested that children who had a temperament at odds with that of the parents should be linked with a more temperamentally compatible foster parent. In spite of the allure to many parents and children to be free of their blood relations, the result, as Cassidy wrote, would have been "millions of children and parents scurrying around the countryside, all trying to find the right match" (1982: 56).

Marijuana

Mead's position on the decriminalization of marijuana was misunderstood. With her knowledge of cultures in which drugs had a variety of uses, she was against the outright puritanical rejection of them. If little fuss were made about marijuana, she reasoned, young people would be less inclined to move on to illegal harder drugs. Mead was more worried about people being able to obtain a variety of prescription drugs from different doctors who did not communicate with each other, with possible lethal combinations prescribed.

Many people, because of her position on marijuana and her frankness on other issues, were incensed. The governor of Florida called her a "dirty old woman" (as cited in Howard 1984: 390).

In Summary

Although a few ideas were misunderstood or not well targeted, Mead recognized the problems in American society, especially those within families, and tried to remedy them with originality and creativity. Since she wrote and spoke "for the record" for fifty years, Mead was bound to founder sometimes, but the breadth and depth of her knowledge was amazing, as was her ability to communicate her ideas to the general public. She expressed herself authoritatively about many subjects beyond the scope of this book: aging fashionably, the role of grandparents in modern society, body language, education, population growth, energy, and ekistics (the study of human settlements and city planning), all areas into which anthropologists had not previously ventured.

HOW ANTHROPOLOGISTS VIEWED MEAD

Regardless of Mead's popular success, many colleagues only benevolently tolerated her. On the one hand, they gave tacit approval to her because they recognized that the growth of departments of anthropology (in other words, their own jobs) was in great part due to her efforts. On the other hand, they considered Mead's catering to the public an abomination.

Mead's first publisher, William Morrow, cautioned her in a June 20, 1928, letter that she would face ramifications from colleagues by publishing in the popular press, although he personally had no objections to her request to write an article for the magazine *Smart Set*. Mead paid attention to Morrow's advice and chose to publicize *Coming of Age in Samoa* by writing for the *Nation* and *American Mercury*, but later she had no qualms about writing for mainstream periodicals like *TV Guide* and *Redbook*.

Mead realized, she paid a price by publishing in the popular press and by writing with a more readable, less academic style for professional journals. Her writing was dismissed by many colleagues as belonging to the "rustling-of-the-wind-in-the-palm-trees" school of anthropology.[2] When Robert Lowie, a prominent anthropologist, wrote to Mead to request comments on Boas, Mead indicated surprise in her April 8, 1956, reply at being asked. "I have got accustomed to being treated as anthropologically non-existent" (Library of Congress: c). An anthropologist told Mead's friend and colleague William Mitchell that Mead's name was never mentioned during the eight years he studied at Cambridge. Mead had once "mused rather ruefully" (Mitchell 1996: 131) to him about lack of acknowledgment of her work from her colleagues.

Mead also irritated anthropologists because many assumed the fees she received for speaking engagements were making her wealthy; however, Mead left a modest estate after taxes of $222,081.67 (Howard 1984: 427), or about $603,000 in 2001 dollars. Like her mother, Mead contributed to causes in which she believed, both large and small. For example, because protecting the environment was important to her, she gave a week's lecture fees to the Scientific Institute of Public Information to further their campaign on the use of biodegradable goods. One organization to which she gave generous donations anonymously was the American Anthropological Association (AAA). Michael Salovesh, president of the Association of Senior Anthropologists (2000–2002), a division of the AAA, writes:

> Margaret Mead provided financial support to anthropology students, to established scholars, and to anthropological organizations out of a special fund she paid for out of her own pocket. Her gifts filled the gaps in the minimal support that was available to students seeking research grant support. If she heard of a student about to go to the field where the research could be improved by the use of a tape recorder or a video camera, Margaret would provide the necessary tools as a grant-in-aid gift. She sometimes found students who, in her opinion, needed to make a visit of a month or so to the place where they wanted to do more extended work. Margaret would pay for the short trip whenever she thought a student would be able to use information from that visit to write a first-class grant proposal that would bring support for longer fieldwork and a writeup period. Margaret's fund also provided small-grant support for airline tickets that brought international scholars to the U.S. for special conferences, or took U.S. scholars to conferences in other countries.
>
> The American Anthropological Association went through a major financial crisis in the 1960s. The association was deeply in debt and the financial records were a complete mess. All Fellows of the Association were asked for a one-time assessment of $25 apiece to help dig the organization out of its hole. Many of us who were not yet Fellows also contributed $25 apiece to help rescue the AAA from its nearly bankrupt condition. What saved the day, however, was a gift of $25,000 from an anonymous donor. The donor was Margaret Mead, who insisted on the strictest anonymity for her contribution.
>
> Whenever Margaret's special fund was getting low, she'd call her booking agent to arrange for a speaking tour—and all the profits from the trip would be paid directly into Margaret's fund. What the public always saw on these trips was a dynamic speaker with a wondrous gift for interaction with her audiences. She did not allow them to see how tremendously draining it was for her to maintain that public persona. Behind the scenes, though, she made sure that she normally would not have to wear her public face for more than four or five hours at a stretch. She insisted on scheduling mid-day breaks that

allowed her to retire, alone and uninterrupted, to a convenient hotel room for at least a couple of hours before having to reappear later in the day.

Most anthropologists don't know about Margaret's fund and the good work it has done. Most of us always knew that Margaret's fees when she was on a speaking tour were quite high for their time. (I think I recall that her fee for a speaking appearance would be $2500 to $5000 all the way back in the mid1960s. She'd often make paid appearances at two different institutions on the same day.) Because so few knew about Margaret's fund, there were lots of people within the larger family of anthropologists who were miffed at what they saw as Margaret's self-commercialization. They were particularly unhappy that when she was on a speaking tour, Margaret rarely made any accommodations for "extra" (read "unpaid") appearances before anthropology departments or student groups. She was well aware of that current of resentment, but she absolutely refused to squelch it by talking about what she did with her fund.[3] (M. Salovesh, personal correspondence, December 17, 2002)

As a point of reference, Mead's initial contribution of $25,000 had the 2001 purchasing power of approximately $140,500 (http://eh.net/ehresources/howmuch).

SHEPHERD'S CROOK

In 1960 Mead slipped on grease in a friend's kitchen and broke her ankle for the fourth time. Reluctant to use a common cane, she purchased her first shepherd's crook, a walking stick, or cudgel, as she called it, that reached her shoulder and had a forked top. Combined with the long cloaks she favored, Mead cut an unforgettable figure with her crook.

These two symbols not only hid walk and weight but provided a dramatic and unique persona. She circumvented later physical problems, like dozing off easily and dyslexia, but one major problem was deafness. Hearing aids in the 1970s were unable to filter out background noise, so being in a crowded room was difficult.

By 1977, physical problems were taking their toll and her last years were discouraging for friends and fans. Older members of audiences felt disappointed and sad that Mead was rambling, seemingly without a prepared speech, and young people were disappointed that their idol snarled. Biographer Jane Howard described an incident in June 1977 at which she was present. Graduate students had prepared an exhibit on families and were thrilled that Mead was going to view it and, they assumed, praise their efforts and encourage them. Instead she was grumpy and sarcastic. Howard summarized: "Her lifelong tendency to come straight to the point, a blunt and refreshing impatience, turned now to plain, and sometimes astonishing, rudeness" (1984: 402).

January 1978 was the last month Mead adhered to her busy schedule, even though she was in constant pain from a cancer whose existence she refused to accept. By February, stomach pain and her flagging energy forced the elimination of many activities, including a planned trip to investigate aging in Russia.

DEATH

Mead resisted admitting her imminent death from pancreatic cancer to the public, to her friends, and to herself. It was the same disease that had killed her brother, Richard, in 1975. After receiving unwelcome advice from the traditional medical establishment, Mead began to visit a psychic healer, the Reverend Carmen diBarazza.[4] Mead was open to accepting mysticism, including faith healing, and diBarazza's backrubs, special diet, and motherly warmth seemed to help. She continued to lose weight but felt well enough to attend professional gatherings, including an August conference at Chautauqua Institution in northwestern New York state with ex-spouse Bateson and daughter Bateson, visiting from Iran.

In October Mead began hemorrhaging and was rushed to the hospital, where she died on November 15, 1978, in New York City. Upon Mead's death, her name was a household word, as familiar as names of the biggest sports stars and politicians. Millions of words had been and continue to be written in an attempt to characterize her. She has been called "prolific, outspoken, charismatic, unconventional, provocative, controversial, and brilliant" (Newman 1996: 233). And those adjectives were from just one of the thousands of pages of material describing her and her work. Even her obituary in the *New York Times* admitted to her being "lacerating," but added that she was "more often gentle and witty" (Whitman 1978: D18). The obituary also observed, "Insofar as anyone can be a polymath, Dr. Mead was widely regarded as one" (D18).

Chapter 8

PATTERNS OF PEOPLE, CAREER OF CONTROVERSY

> I remember walking down Amsterdam Avenue with a
> fellow student in the spring of 1925, and seeing two
> people meet, each greeting the other in passing, "Good
> evening! Isn't it a lovely evening?" And we two students
> turned to each other and said in one breath, "Pattern!"
> —Mead, *An Anthropologist at Work* (1959)

The many patterns in Mead's life coalesced around circles of people. An outer circle held those whose lives she touched, even though impersonally. The middle circle contained a multitude of friends, students, members of organizations to which she belonged, and colleagues. The inner circle was composed of family and a few close friends to whom she opened various parts of her life.

THE OUTER CIRCLE

Mead loved her fans and welcomed her fame. As Sey Chassler, editor-in-chief of *Redbook* magazine, wrote in the preface to a collection of her essays originally published in his magazine, "Margaret Mead loved to be loved" (Mead and Métraux 1980: 8). She said when she was young that she worried she would never be recognized, but speaking in 1973 she said recognition was no longer a concern. She was so recognizable at airports that signing autographs interrupted a quick sandwich. An airport customs agent checked every item of hers meticulously, not because he expected contraband but because he knew his wife would want to know what Margaret Mead took on a trip. After landing, airline pilots told her they were honored she flew with them.

Mead loved the adulation and she also loved to talk to people. Once, when traveling, she declined the opportunity to fly over a glacier; she had little interest in scenery and there would be no one to whom she could talk. Almost as huge a thrill as talking was communicating via the written word. The mail Mead received each day weighed from ten to fifteen pounds. From schoolchildren to the luminaries of anthropology, people wrote her and she responded. Mead was "a singular and uniquely charismatic public intellectual" (Rapp 2001).

THE MIDDLE CIRCLE

Mead enjoyed remaining in touch with a long list of family, personal friends, and acquaintances. Anthropologist William Mitchell, also a friend and onetime student, described her network as "spanning continents, cultures, professions and ages" (1996: 129). This network was like the knitting she enjoyed—individual strands that looped and connected and gave texture to the fabric of her life. Mead communicated with all these kith and kin via holiday cards, notes, and visits.

When Cathy was young, Margaret began sending Christmas cards with a photograph of mother and daughter, or a photograph taken on a trip. In later years granddaughter Vanni appeared in the photographs. Eventually the list climbed to 521 addressees, all cards personally signed. She also frequently jotted notes; friends remembered her writing to extend sympathy for a loss in their life.

When traveling, Mead preferred to visit people with whom she could talk and share meals and who provided transportation to events on her very tight and synchronized professional schedule. She even visited Fortune's family, her former in-laws, while in New Zealand and she loved to visit Cincinnati, a city that held friends and also relatives from both sides of her family. Mead's mother died in 1950 and her father, who mellowed as he grew older, died six years later; Mead had visited them often in Philadelphia.

When Mead was in New York, she preferred having friends for dinner to eating alone and always enjoyed cooking. Although she readily accepted convenience foods, Margaret made creative salads.

She insisted on several kinds of lettuce, capers, pimento, herbs, finely chopped garlic, salt and pepper, a tiny bit of mustard, and two measures of oil to one measure of three or more different types of vinegar. The entire dinner was put on a tea trolley and wheeled to the table and she tossed the salad prior to serving it at the end of the meal. Although she relished cooking, Mead did not like to clean up and stacked dirty dishes in a teetering pyramid, awaiting the arrival of cleaning help.

A social reformer and consummate extrovert, Mead was an active member of numerous organizations, including the American Anthropological Association (AAA), the American Association for the Advancement of Science (AAAS), the American Association of University Women (AAUW), Planned Parenthood, the United Nations (UN), the Episcopal Church, and the World Council of Churches. She served as president of both the AAA and the AAAS.

United Nations

A single organization embracing all the world's countries appealed to Mead theoretically, and the United Nations included third-world countries in its positive efforts to deal with children's health problems, nutrition, population control, environment, and issues important to her. Mead attended UN-sponsored conferences, and people in various offices were delighted when she called on department heads. She wrote the preface to and edited *Cultural Patterns and Technical Change* for the UN Educational, Scientific, and Cultural Organization (UNESCO), a small volume that dealt with how to introduce modernized methods for healthcare, agriculture, and education "so that the cultures will be disrupted as little as possible" (1963a: 15–16).

In speeches encouraging support of the UN, Mead emphasized the need for clean air, a need that transcended national boundaries and an undertaking that meant the elimination of cheap gasoline in the United States and major changes in US energy policy. Given the US government's reluctance to make Mead-recommended changes in energy policy, perhaps she felt prayer could prevail. The Reverend Roger L. Shinn remembered meeting with Mead to discuss energy, ecology, and social justice. Mead argued issues and then suddenly said, "Prayer does not use up any artificial energy, it doesn't burn up any fossil fuel, it doesn't pollute" (as cited in Shinn 1978: 306).

Work in the Episcopal Church

Mead sought solace in Episcopal services throughout her life and, unlike many scientists, had a "deep commitment to Christianity" (Bateson 1984: 100). She often interrupted a project of her own to serve on a committee for the World Council of Churches or the National Council of Churches.

Both Margaret and Catherine Bateson were in favor of ordination of women priests but preferred the 1928 *Book of Common Prayer*. Mead felt a woman should serve as priest, minister, or rabbi; the only problem was defining her role, since a woman brought other gifts to the position than those traditionally contributed by men. "What is needed," she wrote in a 1975 article, "is a new concern for what a gifted woman can contribute . . . without denying or destroying what is male and valuable" (Mead and Métraux 1980: 83).

Despite her preference for the existing *Book of Common Prayer*, Mead worked on a committee to make revisions in the sections on baptism and confirmation. Particular lines cannot be traced to her, but she missed only one meeting in six years of work and was not the member-in-absentia other committee members expected.

Although the Episcopal Church was right for her, Mead, not one to proselytize, encouraged people to make their own religion choices. "A child without religious experience shared with trusted persons who are religious may grow to adulthood either incapable of religious faith or uncritically susceptible to intemperate religious appeals," she wrote in a March 1966 *Redbook* article. She labeled both of these "incapacitating alternatives" (1979: 177).

Conferences

Mead began a lifelong love affair with conferences when she attended the 1924 conference of the British Association for the Advancement of Science. She was a presenter at innumerable conferences great and small and attended hundreds of others. She even spoke at conferences on the merits of conferences and collaborated with photographer-anthropologist Paul Byers on *The Small Conference: An Innovation in Communication* (1968), in which they examined the dynamics of participants' interaction through sequences of photographs. Little wonder Mary Catherine Bateson recalled her mother saying "a really successful conference is one in which the intensity is so great that you feel as if you are falling in love" (Bateson 1984: 226).

Mead fervently believed that conferences were crucial for networking with colleagues and getting the latest information from the people who conducted the research. While many of her fellow anthropologists chatted with colleagues, Mead was present at all the scheduled sessions she could find time to attend; she could, she believed, listen to someone and gain more information in a few minutes than she could reading the research when it was eventually published.

Some of the speakers may have wished Mead had not attended their sessions. With her long cloak and walking stick, her appearance was described in a *New Yorker* article as suggesting "a middle-aged and extraordinarily intelligent Valkyrie" (Sargeant 1961: 32). Although she didn't literally select warriors to be slain and escort them to Valhalla, she could instantly wither people with her opinions. Mead had two techniques when she disagreed with a remark, whether it was made from the podium or the floor. First, she rose to her feet, faced the audience, and "pounded her criticisms home with forked stick and tongue" (Grinager 1999: 122). Her other technique was to stay seated and say "Rubbish" repeatedly, raising her voice each time she spoke it.

"Have fun!"

On his way to the 1978 conference of the American Anthropological Association in Los Angeles, William Mitchell visited Mead's hospital room. Mitchell took the hands of the tiny figure wrapped in a quilt, eyes closed, body drugged to stave off the pain of cancer. She smiled broadly, he reported, and then, "When I told her where I was going, she pressed my hands and said, 'Have fun!'" (Mitchell 1996: 132). To Margaret Mead, fun was what conferences were.

Almost as if she willed it, and certainly it would have pleased her if she realized it, Mead passed away on the opening day of the AAA conference, November 15, 1978. Her death, since her illness had been kept relatively quiet, shocked the audience. Nancy Scheper-Hughes, professor of anthropology at the University of California, Berkeley, described the announcement of Mead's death as creating an awkward silence in the auditorium. Once the official announcement was made, the conference buzzed with the news (1984).

THE INNER CIRCLE

In the book *The Cooperative Collaborative Process*, which summarizes positive, significant research findings about cooperation and collaboration and provides techniques for use, the authors write, "When we share our knowledge and skills the sum is greater than the parts. Knowledge is like friendship. The more you share the more you get back" (Mainzer et al. 1996). This combination of friendship and collaboration was a concept Mead valued. After her initial fieldwork, she always preferred working as a team.

Mead's first and most rewarding collaborative friendship was with Ruth Benedict. Their teamwork was not focused on a single product but on helping each other work through individual projects in an ongoing process. Mead wrote in *Blackberry Winter* that when Benedict died, they had each read everything the other had written. No one but Benedict had so completely critiqued her work.

Mead honored Benedict by writing an *American Anthropologist* obituary that ended, "We shall not look upon her like again" (Mead 1949b: 463), a slight change to the words spoken by Shakespeare's Hamlet.[1] She ultimately graced Ruth's memory by writing two biographies, *An Anthropologist at Work: Writings of Ruth Benedict* (1973a) and *Ruth Benedict* (1974a).

Mead was always direct to acknowledge the depth of her professional relationship with Benedict, but not the breadth of her personal relationship. In the early years of the twentieth century females were encouraged to develop warm, close friendships with other women, partly because such relationships would prepare them for marriage and partly because most people envisioned a women's sexuality only in terms of dependence on a male partner. In the 1920s, intimacies between middle-class women were common, since the attitude of the entire era, especially in cosmopolitan cities, was one of tolerance. As women eventually grew more sexually independent, homophobia among the general population forced personal discretion and Mead refused to be labeled so far as her sexual orientation. When asked to compare her relationships with Benedict and her husbands, Margaret replied, "[I] put my relationship to Ruth and my relationship to my husbands in the same box—whole relationships to adults" (as cited in Lapsley 1999: 77).

In addition to documentation of a lesbian relationship presented by Hilary Lapsley in *Margaret Mead and Ruth Benedict: The Kinship of Women*, Mary Catherine Bateson, after examining her mother's private papers and piecing together information, believed that they were involved sexually. She wrote that Ruth was one of the two people Margaret "loved most fully and abidingly, exploring all the possibilities of personal and intellectual closeness" (Bateson 1984: 140). How long into their lives the sexual side of their love for each other continued "will most likely never be known" (Lapsley 1999: 330).

Since Mead peeked into so many sexual relationships, looking into hers does not seem unfair, but one should consider that Mead's sexual side was one small component of a rich, productive life.

Collaboration with Métraux

A professional collaboration with Rhoda Métraux began in 1942 when she was Mead's research assistant. Eventually Métraux's work as coauthor and editor enabled Mead's advice and views to touch a generation of women readers of *Redbook* magazine. The monthly columns, written for sixteen years, were based on Mead's collection of questions after her speeches and were then revised and refined by Métraux. Richard Warms, anthropology professor at Southwest Texas State University, calls the columns "unprecedented in the history of anthropology and, as far as I know, never duplicated. Any collaboration that goes on for as long as theirs did is surely spectacular and worthy of note" (R. Warms, personal communication, March 12, 2002).

Their personal friendship lasted even longer. Rhoda Métraux was married to anthropologist Alfred Métraux but after they divorced and the Franks, friends with whom Mead and her daughter, Cathy, had shared homes for many years, moved to Boston in 1955, Rhoda and Margaret lived together and Rhoda's support, with help from Haitian housekeeper Tulia Sampeur, allowed Mead to focus on her career and rear Cathy, then a teenager, along with Daniel, Rhoda's son. Despite personal differences in later years, Rhoda and Margaret shared the same address for twenty-three years, longer than Mead lived with three husbands.

The question remains open as to whether they were lovers. Mead wrote in a January 1975 article for *Redbook* magazine, "The time has come, I think, when we must recognize bisexuality as a normal form of human behavior" (Mead and Métraux 1980: 269). Bisexuality was not new, she said, but widening the awareness and acceptance of the human capacity to love is.

Family Connections

Mead's relationship with her sister Elizabeth Steig, the only sibling who outlived her, seemed to strengthen in later life and Mead partially wrote *Blackberry Winter* while staying with Elizabeth (Grinager 1999: 204).[2] Whether for actual or embraced family, Mead tried never to miss major life occasions, like weddings and baptisms, and she personally purchased Christmas gifts for her many nieces, nephews, godchildren, and other children with whom she was close.

Although Mead's ex-husbands no longer belonged to her inner circle, they held a unique place in her life and she remained in contact with them, their new wives, and her past in-laws. Mead had the most contact with Bateson, probably because of their shared offspring but possibly because she continued to have strong feelings for him. Fortune, with whom she had the least contact, lived in England, and Cressman and Bateson moved to the West Coast of the United States. While the primary reason for their moves may not have been to escape Margaret, they were probably happy not to be in near proximity. When

Bateson was invited to a party while still living in New York, the host said Margaret would not be there. He replied that her network would be. Working in the same field as an ex-spouse surely made their situations difficult, especially since Mead was a celebrity whose voice was often heard emanating from radio or television, whose persona was obvious at conferences, and whose words frequently appeared in print.

Similarly, being her daughter brought benefits but difficulties. Little wonder Catherine Bateson became an anthropologist—or specialized in an area of anthropology to which neither parent had background or connection. When she and Margaret traveled to Israel in the summer of 1956, Catherine decided to remain for a year to finish high school and then return to the United States to attend college. Bateson appreciated her mother's encouraging her to go her own way in life. After Bateson's 1960 marriage to John Barkev Kassarjian, the couple lived and worked in the Philippines and Iran, so actual time together, as when Catherine was growing up and Mead traveled, was limited, although a "mental intimacy" was reported to have existed between Margaret and Catherine (Howard 1984: 246).

Mead's granddaughter, Sevanne Margaret Kassarjian, was born in 1969 and called Vanni. Although Mead had worked almost half a century with kinship systems, she was thrilled that through no action of her own she was biologically linked to a new life. Like any grandmother, Mead traveled with multiple pictures of Vanni and showed them to hosts in whose homes she stayed.

The circles of people surrounding Margaret in late 1978 made Margaret's death a very difficult situation for Catherine. The Kassarjians, then in Iran during the midst of revolution, found their lives in turmoil. As Margaret's illness progressed, Catherine flew with Vanni to spend two weeks with her, "a painful and disturbing time" (Bateson 1984: 271), both because Margaret was physically unable to organize and control the situation and because she denied death was imminent. Catherine found "a continual conundrum of missionaries and cannibals around the bed and in the hallway" (271) and worried that her mother, by "self-deception" in denying the severity of her illness, was leaving herself open to "deception and exploitation" (274) from others.

When looking over her mother's personal effects returned by the hospital after her death, Catherine remembered warmly that Margaret had kept a faded and worn Mother's Day card she sent her in 1971 and family photographs (Bateson 1984: 118).

Other Close Friends

Other close friends throughout Mead's life included Marie Eichelberger, Larry and Mary Frank, and Sara Ullman. Marie Eichelberger cleared Mead's path from their days in college until Mead's death. She archived photographs and papers for her. She handled Margaret's finances. She packed a medical bag for Mead to take on fieldwork; reviving an unconscious child by floating ammonia under his nose while in New Guinea was one of numerous times Mead's reaching into her bag impressed onlookers. Eichelberger turned her apartment over to Bateson and Mead upon their return from Bali. She supplied threaded needles for Mead's sewing box. She made large aprons for Margaret to cover office clothes and sewed tags with "Margaret Mead" onto the corners of handkerchiefs Margaret bought by the dozen. After retirement from a career as a social worker, she worked in Mead's office at the American Museum of Natural History. She was Cathy Bateson's godmother and shopped for her clothes during her childhood. The apartment of "Aunt Marie," as Mary Catherine Bateson called her, was the one in which she spent the first months of life and the one from which she left to start her married life; Bateson called it "my second and most constant home throughout my childhood" (1984: 16). Hilary Lapsley described the multiple roles of Eichelberger by saying that until Mead's death Marie "continued to perform homemaking, secretarial, and maternal tasks for the friend to whom she had devoted her life" (1999: 308).

Mary and Larry Frank shared homes and lives with Mead and Cathy. In her memoirs, Catherine, who called them Aunt Mary and Uncle Larry, remembered that Larry was concerned about nutrition and that, long before the widespread use of vitamins, he placed little glass dishes containing various types of nutritional supplements beside each person's breakfast setting. As in Margaret's youth, the two families organized plays with homemade costumes and, to her mother's exasperation, Gregory changed Shakespeare's words even though he left the meaning intact.

Not only were their personal lives compatible, but Larry's professional interests meshed with Margaret's. He was involved in the education of children and young adults, but his broader agenda was interdisciplinary work in human growth and development. He was a valuable professional friend too, because he was a "philanthropoid" (Grinager 1999: 39). When Patricia Grinager quizzed him about being a philanthropoid, he replied mischievously that it is someone hired by a philanthropic foundation to spend its money. At his funeral in 1968, Margaret praised Larry as someone "who used foundations the way the Lord meant them to be used" (as cited by Howard 1984: 244).

Sara and Alfred Ullman lived near Mead and the Franks, and the families were close during Cathy's childhood years. Mead's atypical problem-solving skills always helped her fit her dual lives into a grueling schedule. When Cathy was older, Margaret paid for Sara's housecleaner. In return, Sara picked up Cathy with her daughter, Martha, also an only child, after school and spent time with both girls. Several evenings a week, Margaret cooked special dinners for herself and Cathy, to make up in quality what was lost in quantity of time together.

Close but Not Personal

Mead's interactions with friends had an agenda; they were not simply casual meetings to enjoy each other's company. Because she traveled so much, meetings tended to be intense reunions. Howard reported Mead saying that even though she lived with Rhoda, there was usually an "agenda" and there was "no time for casualness" (as cited in Howard 1984: 296) with friends.

Despite Mead's intensity in relationships, she was usually sensitive and considerate. Barbara Honeyman Heath Roll recalled that on a visit Mead not only engaged a hotel room for her but personally inspected it and left roses and her favorite drink with a welcoming note. Patricia Grinager credited Mead, eager to match people with professional positions, with practically running a personal employment agency. While idleness was not something in which Margaret Mead indulged, generosity of self was.

CRITICISMS AND CONTROVERSIES

Despite Mead's loving to be loved, she invited controversy. In the mid-1990s William Mitchell wrote, "During her life, Mead was, as she continues to be, a controversial figure" (1996: 130). She has been blamed for the general permissiveness of today's twenty-first-century young people and widely blamed for today's lax sexual morals and loss of religious ethics. A 1999 article by James Lee, published in the *St. Croix Review*, directly linked Mead to the 1999 shootings of students at Columbine High School in Colorado. Her name has been used to discredit today's teachers and to make a case for teaching phonics in the schools.

While some of these criticisms seem ridiculous and require a stretch, Louise Newman wrote that Mead envisioned herself as an objective scientist whose work was "politically detached, morally neutral, theoretically valid, and empirically sound" (1996: 254). On each of these grounds a rational look is warranted at criticisms leveled against Mead.

Political Detachment

Although some biographers have seen Mead as apolitical, she often played a role behind the scenes. Mead kept her top-security clearance during the 1950s and maintained ties to government projects during the Cold War.

In the 1950s, many Americans were disturbed by the manner in which Senator Joseph McCarthy crusaded to rid government agencies and the entertainment world of communists, often through guilt by association. His hearings, replete with insults, insinuation, and intimidation, caused many anthropologists to shrink from government service. Those who remained left during the 1960s when turmoil embroiled the country—student demonstrations against the war in Vietnam, marches for civil rights, concerns about the worldwide rise of communism and nuclear warfare.

In a 1973 article titled "Changing Styles of Anthropological Work," Mead referred to anthropologists working for the government when she wrote, "The contradiction between a willingness during World War II to become involved and a disinclination to become involved later has not yet been resolved" (1973b: 2). Mead's reference was possibly to the well-known 1964–1965 instance of mutual cooperation between anthropologists and government intelligence, dubbed Project Camelot, which did not involve Mead, or to personal difficulties during a 1971 dispute within the American Anthropological Association (AAA) over what is now called the "Thailand controversy."

In the 1960s several anthropologists were involved in assisting US intelligence in Thailand, with the possibility that their information would be used in counterinsurgency activities and that many innocent villagers would suffer or be killed. Members of the recently created AAA ethics committee publicly reprimanded the anthropologists, whose careers were then in jeopardy. Two issues were involved: "One ethical dilemma involved activities that may have been used to physically harm the people studied; the other had the potential for ruining people's reputations" (Wakin 1992: 161).

AAA executive board members unanimously agreed on Margaret Mead to chair the "Ad Hoc Committee to Evaluate the Controversy Concerning Anthropological Activities in Thailand," a name soon shortened to "Mead Committee." What was already a murky situation became worse as the committee accumulated voluminous amounts of materials. "The Mead Committee Report itself cited 212 requests for information, 67 responses, and about 6000 pages of material" (Wakin 1992: 203). The report, glossing over ethics issues, vindicated the anthropologists involved in intelligence activities and condemned two members of the ethics committee for their public statements.

The Mead Committee wanted its report to be distributed at the annual convention, but when it was mailed prior to the event, as was typically done, members were then primed to rebut and reject the report, a personal rebuke to Mead. Although she had agreed to forward the committee's vast amounts of material to the AAA, Mead brusquely responded by saying she destroyed the documents. Eric Wakin, reporting the aftermath of the acrimonious controversy in *Anthropology Goes to War*, wrote, "Mead's response could hardly *not* [italics in original] be called a 'fit of pique.' . . . Even if there was no damning information . . . collected by the Mead Committee, by destroying it, the end result is an unanswerable curiosity, which can never be satisfied through legitimate scholarly access to the documents" (1993: 230–231). Whether Mead was supporting the involvement of anthropologists in covert government activities or was simply angry at what she perceived as a personal humiliation cannot be determined.

David Price, chair of the Department of Sociology and Cultural Anthropology at St. Martin's College, Lacey, Washington, summarizes the situation by saying, "Mead was a complex person, but her involvement in suppressing an honest report of the facts of the Thailand Affair is very troubling." This issue remains relevant in today's world. "Ongoing relationships between anthropologists and the CIA continue to raise concerns about anthropologists working for intelligence agencies" (D. Price, personal communication, February 16, 2002).

Moral Neutrality

In summarizing Mead's contributions, Robert Cassidy, author of numerous articles and author and editor of several books, wrote, "In a lifetime of writing, Mead brought considerable intelligence and humanity to the discussion of religious and moral issues" (1982: 151). Mead, like Kroeber, a Boas student who became an eminent anthropologist and helped found the University of California at Berkley's anthropology department, Benedict, and other Boasians, adamantly opposed racism and, within the constraints of mid-twentieth-century American mores, carried Boas's attitudes about racial equality forward. Her specific views on racial issues within the United States, however, are usually reduced to opinions she expressed in a dialogue with essayist and novelist James Baldwin. In 1970, Baldwin, an African-American who lived much of his life in France to escape racial prejudice in the United States, and Mead audiotaped three sessions published the next year as *A Rap on Race*. Both Baldwin and Mead tended to ramble and sometimes spoke contentiously during the taping. Mead said that race should be ignored and cultural differences recognized. Baldwin argued that history should not be seen as a way of avoiding responsibility and guilt, for slavery required atonement, but Mead was adamant about responsibility only for her own actions and considered herself, and by extension other people, responsible for the present and future, not the past. Mead called some of Baldwin's comments "Just plain fiddlesticks!" (as cited in Howard 1984: 399).

Mead was later relieved when Baldwin was positive about her contribution to the dialogue. Comments on *A Rap on Race* varied from "constructive" (Cassidy 1982: 134) to "her lowest moment," the latter from friend Ned O'Gorman (as cited in Howard 1984: 399).

Mead's legacy in other moral matters is inconsistent. In *Anthropological Theory: An Introductory History*, McGee and Warms write, "All humans are ethnocentric to one degree or another" (1996: 8) and Mead the scientist, like other anthropologists of her era, clearly looked at the cultures she visited through the lens of white Western society. The people of Samoa and Papua New Guinea, in particular, have been angry at Mead about issues involving problems of language and money. Samoans rebelled against Mead's hedonistic view of their culture, but Mead was adamant that *Coming of Age in Samoa* remain as she wrote it; however, she strongly stated in the preface to later editions that she was writing about Samoa and the United States as they existed from 1926 to 1928.

Papua New Guineans have disagreed with Mead's version of their history. Mead wrote in *New Lives for Old* that the story of the Pere people was "the story of a people without history" (1956: 21). The Pere perceive having a history, but not one fashioned by Western world standards. They also resent some terminology in Mead's books that by twenty-first-century standards seems abrasive; for example, *primitive* is considered pejorative today but in Mead's day referred to a culture with no written language.

Another concern has been Mead's omission of problems. In 1953 Mead ignored the racism involved in Papua New Guineans working in low-status menial jobs at whites-only clubs. The role of an anthropologist is not to change the society he or she is observing, but neither is it to focus only on positive aspects. Mead herself recognized what she termed her "life-long optimism" (1979: 276), which caused her to gloss over the negative.

Nicholas von Hoffman and Garry Trudeau, *Doonesbury* cartoonist, wrote in a satirical book skewering America and Samoa, "Anthropology is unique among exploitive enterprises inasmuch as it manages to leave intact the very commodity it extracts" (1979: 52).

Papua New Guineans became angry when Mead did indeed leave their country intact. Mead, they believed, benefited monetarily and with increased popularity from writing about their country, but she did not share her financial rewards. In 1986 Nahau Rooney, by then a Papua New Guinean politician and activist, said that when she and other students at the University of Papua New Guinea asked Mead for consulting help to establish a provincial government and a monetary contribution to carry on their work, she provided little of either. "Here we are contributing to her lectures and giving her world status and yet she did not contribute anything. We were making her famous" (Foerstel and Gilliam 1992: 44). In Mead's defense, South Pacific societies have reaped benefits (as well as problems) from publicity generated by Mead's books.

Theoretical Validity

Mead concluded in *Coming of Age in Samoa* that culture, not biology, determined the degree of stress felt by adolescent young women. Mead's was not an empirical study that relied on comparative data gathered in both countries; it was a descriptive study that relied on her finding that Samoan young women had little stress. This finding provided the negative instance to prove the theory from data collected by assessment instruments she devised and by notes gathered through observation.

When *Coming of Age in Samoa* was published, Mead's close colleagues were unqualified in their praise and there was general support for the book in the scientific community outside Columbia University. The reviewer for *American Anthropologist*, the discipline's flagship journal, was positive, "in spite of sensible reservations regarding some of her unqualified generalizations" (Orans 1996: 3), reservations that continue to exist about much of her work. It was on other grounds, however, that Mead's work received the greatest scrutiny from her foremost critic, Derek Freeman.

Derek Freeman was born in New Zealand in 1916 and studied philosophy and psychology at Victoria University. From 1940 to 1943 he worked and conducted fieldwork in western Samoa, where he learned the language and was adopted as a son by a *tulafale*, or talking chief.

His credentials include a doctorate from Cambridge University and, from 1955 until he retired, he was professor of anthropology and department chair at Australian National University. Returning from a sabbatical to study at the London Institute of Psychoanalysis, he reread *Coming of Age in Samoa* and was so disturbed by its exclusion of a biological perspective to adolescence that during 1966 and 1967 he returned to Samoa to find documentation to refute Mead's research. During his long career, Freeman produced substantial work not related to what is now known as the "Mead-Freeman controversy," but he is primarily remembered for the latter.

Since scientific work necessitates revisiting and revising past research, Lowell Holmes, a student at Northwestern University, went to Ta'u in 1954 to investigate how Samoan life would look twenty-five years later to a married man. Although he found areas in which he disagreed with Mead, he generally concurred with her findings.

Mead and Freeman had several communications prior to her death, but it was not until 1983 that Freeman's book *Margaret Mead and Samoa: The Making and Unmaking of an Anthropological Myth* was published, followed in 1999 by *The Fateful Hoaxing of Margaret Mead*.

Harvard University Press provided an advance media blitz for Freeman's first book. The publicity resulted in a page-one story in the *New York Times*, multiple television appearances on Freeman's American tour, and articles highlighting the disputes, both between the people involved—Freeman versus Mead—and between the philosophies—nature versus nurture. Anthropologists quickly recognized that the heart of the controversy was not Mead's long-ago research that she conducted in 1925–1926, but "Freeman's critique, [which] with its avowed intention of giving the biological a greater role, was seen as reactionary and racist" (Orans 1996: 6–7). While Mead was perceived as substantiating a theory they endorsed, Freeman's theory was viewed by the average anthropologist as abhorrent.

Freeman criticized Mead on a number of issues:

Mead preplanned findings to support cultural relativism. Luther Cressman, who would have been privy to planning a predetermined result, wrote that neither Mead nor Boas anticipated what she would find (1988: 115). Boasian anthropologists did not falsify data, but they had what Richard Warms calls "a disturbing knack" for finding confirmation that supported cultural over biological reasons for behavior (R. Warms, personal communication, March 16, 2002).

Mead overemphasized culture and neglected the role of biology as an influence on behavior. Some anthropologists said Mead included information about nature without stressing it, but the fact remains that Mead came down mightily for nurture.

Mead spent too little time in the field to collect sufficient data. Although those who have reviewed her field notes on Samoa and other cultures commend her for diligent, thorough, and rapid collection of data, Mead's actual data-collection time was a brief four to five months. Mead, probably recognizing the brevity of her fieldwork, stretched both the time she was there and the time she spent collecting data.[3]

Mead was not proficient in the language. This is probably true, given her difficulty in quickly learning the Samoan language, although field notes indicate she also collected information from informants and through an interpreter. Freeman claims misspellings are evidence of her limited facility with Samoan, but spelling in her native language never concerned Mead. If Mead is guilty of a language problem in *Coming of Age in Samo*a, it is hyperbole.

Mead depicts most Samoan adolescents as freely participating in premarital sex. Freeman disagreed. One of Freeman's most publicized arguments in his second book came from a filmed 1988 interview with Fa'apua'a, a taupou, or ceremonial virgin, who, with Fofoa, traveled with Mead to visit a village at the other end of Ta'u and also some outlying islands, admitted she and the deceased Fofoa had hoaxed Mead by telling fibs about their sex life. Since the two women at the time Mead conducted her research lived in another area of the island and since none of Mead's field notes attribute information to the women who allegedly hoaxed Mead, Freeman's claim of a hoax is not supported, but neither can it be judged absolutely wrong.

Mead ignored violence in Samoan life. Because Mead focused on the young women, there was no reason for her to report on any problems among adults. Freeman presents a picture of Samoa while Mead was there as far from carefree, with numerous examples of violence.

In analyzing the last two contentions made by Freeman, the reaction of many anthropologists could be summarized that "Derek Freeman is more correct with respect to Samoan aggression, but that Mead was more correct with respect to Samoan sexuality" (Scheper-Hughes 1984: 90).

Empirical Soundness

Mead anticipated future analysis of her field notes, not the modus operandi of someone consciously corrupting data or altering material, but a primary problem with the empirical soundness of her data is imprecision with numbers.[4] No matter how the number of villagers and the number of girls interviewed is counted, the numbers do not tally. This problem does not invalidate her information, since anthropologists in the early part of the twentieth century often not only excluded such data but also excluded description of how data were collected.

Mead probably recognized that her statistical methods were lacking. William Fielding Ogburn, Cressman's adviser and Mead's boss in the Department of Sociology at Columbia, was a model of statistical rigor and in a letter to Boas on January 5, 1926, Mead refers to the "Ogburns of science" as possibly being critical of her methods (http://www.sscl.uwo.ca/sociology/mead/Jan5,1926b.htm).

Problems Freeman perceived provided him with sufficient information to manipulate Mead's writings and field notes. As Hilary Lapsley said, he "tortured the data until it confessed (so to speak!)" (H. Lapsley, personal communication, October 12, 2001). Freeman focused so intensely for so long that, rather than a reasonable critic, he appeared to be a curmudgeon whose arrogance was enhanced by hindsight. He did, however, raise issues that have muted Mead's legacy.

Other Criticisms

Although *Coming of Age in Samoa* has been more stringently evaluated, Mead's second best-known book, *Sex and Temperament in Three Primitive Societies*, has had its critics. Almost uniformly reviewers of both books commended Mead's fieldwork but criticized her tendency to excessively generalize. This problem has been compounded by textbook authors, who further oversimplified her conclusions.

Lapsley believes that Mead's "error of judgment" in *Sex and Temperament* was in being too much influenced by the "points of the compass" theory. If Mead had differentiated the characteristics of societies by the point at which they fell along an imaginary line, she would have avoided the pitfall of classifying societies by extremes. Despite this weakness, Mead's descriptions of the cultures, as in *Coming of Age*, make the book "a classic" (Lapsley 1999: 237).

Most attacks on Mead derive from her immense popularity and her use of the bully pulpit to effectively transmit her progressive views. Although her work was spotty in certain areas and her inclination to make sweeping generalizations bothersome, Mead's overall legacy is positive and continues to be diffused throughout twenty-first-century American life.

Chapter 9

WHAT WOULD MARGARET MEAD SAY TODAY?

> The importance of each daily act—rising in the morning
> to the day's tasks, spending an hour explaining to a sick
> child in a hospital how a caterpillar turns into a butterfly,
> sending a few dollars to relieve famine in another part of
> the world—have to be brought into relationship with our
> decisions to build more and more missiles or to consign a
> million tons of grain to one country instead of another.
> —Mead and Heyman, *World Enough* (1975)

Speaking at an April 2001 Barnard College conference to celebrate the centennial anniversary of Margaret Mead's birth, Rayna Rapp, anthropology professor at New York University, challenged the audience to consider, "WWMMS? What Would Margaret Mead Say?" about today's "cultural landscape."

This cultural landscape, Rapp said, is "rapidly expanding its horizons." Changes have been swift in the years since Mead was the world's most celebrated anthropologist. The growth of technology, with its pervasive impact through video cameras, computers, cell phones, and other electronic equipment, has altered everyday life. The United States has been involved in meandering wars without a recognizable enemy but with far-reaching effects on society. Scientific discoveries, especially those involving reproduction and healthcare with the potential for immense changes in the American family, have emerged and are, as Rapp characterized them, "fraught with political significance."

Because Mead felt so fervently and addressed Americans so eloquently on so many issues, a look at topics she addressed necessitates dealing with the expanding landscape and also covering a broad spectrum of subject matter. What would Margaret Mead say today about

159

the world as an extended community, about the leadership role of the United States, about volunteerism and the gap between elders and youngsters, about diversity, and about the role of cultural relativism? What would she tell women about giving birth and young parents about rearing their children? What advice on the teaching-learning process would she have for families and for educators? And would she support the directions scientific inquiry is now taking?

Dana Raphael, a medical anthropologist and friend of Mead's, notes, "The answers she would give are not like anyone else's" (D. Raphael, personal communication, March 23, 2002). With Mead's "extraordinary appetite for cultural innovation" (Rapp: 2001), what *would* Margaret Mead say today?

THE WORLD AS AN EXTENDED COMMUNITY

> **The whole world must become as one city, where all are citizens and all are willing to take responsibility for one another.**
> —Mead and Métraux, A Way of Seeing (1961)

Mead embraced two concepts that are gradually being realized in some ways but yet still seem far from reality in others—the world as a single community and the importance of each individual within the world. Mead did not like the term *global village*, coined by her Canadian friend Marshall McLuhan, who envisioned electronic media unifying people worldwide. People, Mead responded, can't know everyone in the same face-to-face way as those who lived in villages. Her term of preference was "a shared—a simultaneous—world" (Mead 1979: 103).

Although she began her career wanting to save societies before they changed, Mead grew to see technological change as improving people's lives to help them live longer and have an easier existence. She recognized that technology would lead to societal changes and wrote that "innovations in technology and in the form of institutions inevitably bring about alterations in cultural character" (1970a: 48).

Mead worked for years to sow her ideas on creating a shared world and these ideas illustrate how high and wide her thinking went. In a 1965 article in *Daedalus*, Mead deplored the fragmentation of the world and the piecemeal discussion of problems only "as they affect certain groups" (1965b: 135). She suggested a variety of "ways in which experience can more consciously be brought to bear in developing a shared understanding" (151).

In this article and elsewhere, Mead preached and wrote about the need for a universal language. Using one of the major languages that represented a colonial past or was associated with a great power seemed inappropriate. Mary Catherine Bateson, who had married Barkev Kassarjian, an Armenian, suggested the native language of Mead's son-in-law. Mead's subsequently mentioning the idea in speeches made her popular with Armenians, but additional writing and speaking about a single world language did not garner general acceptance.

Although the world of the twenty-first century is connected electronically, living together peaceably remains a problem that eludes a solution, as tribalism continues to fragment the possibility of a shared world. Because of electronic connections, a face-to-face world seems more possible. Mead, speaking in 1965 in a radio interview with Studs Terkel, Pulitzer Prize-winning author best known for his entertaining and insightful radio interviews, said that Americans had gained "more sense of the importance of the individual" than they previously had. She equated the tendency to value each individual's life with the shared grieving possible through instantaneous television reporting.

Mead was specifically referring to the death of President John F. Kennedy, allegedly assassinated by Lee Harvey Oswald in Dallas, Texas, on November 22, 1963. Mesmerized Americans were horrified as the sequence of events played out on television: the motorcade racing to the hospital, wife Jackie's bloodstained suit, Oswald's arrest and subsequent murder in the basement of the Dallas police station by Jack Ruby, the lines of mourners as JFK's body lay in state in the Capitol rotunda, Kennedy's young son John-John saluting as he stood by his father's casket, the horse-drawn caisson carrying Kennedy's body to Arlington Cemetery. Together the nation, joined in mourning by much of the world, grieved as the images flashed onto their television screens. Mead credited the media with personalizing events, as they "were once personalized in the local gossip of a face-to-face community. We are coming to live in a face-to-face world" (Terkel 1993).

This face-to-face world in the twenty-first century includes the Internet along with television. Today's speedy electronic transmission by a variety of technologies instantaneously broadcasts the horror of killing and devastation around the world. Mead wrote, "The basic ethic of 'Thou shalt not kill'—never realized yet except by a handful of prophetic forerunners of a better world—and of 'thou shalt love thy neighbor as thyself' does not change. But times do, and men and women can" (1973c: 291–292). With a sense of the value of human life, hope for problem-solving to eliminate needless pain and killing is possible, but Mead would be forced to agree that this ambitious goal lies in the future.

Mead feared, however, that world leaders would attempt to manipulate the media. "The immense possibilities of modern communications tempt us to believe that we can in some manner control history. . . . Far from waiting for the judgment of history . . . men attempt to shape not only the present but also the future's view of the present" (Mead and Métraux 1970: 91).

WORLD LEADERSHIP

> Our hope today rests not on peace *winning* but on peace-*keeping*.
> —Mead and Métraux, *A Way of Seeing* (1961)

When an interviewer asked Mead in 1958 if the United States was a nation capable of world leadership, she replied that ability is a moot point. A better question, she responded, concerns what kind of world leadership the United States is capable of: "I think we're far more capable of informal world leadership than formal world leadership. General attitudes in this country toward government mean that we're far more able to be friendly, co-operative, and respectful of the rights and capacities of other countries in a private capacity than we are in a public capacity" (Brandon 1969: 168).

Mead's words still ring true. Support abroad for US policies seems to tumble when American action causes other countries to perceive the United States as acting unilaterally like a giant demanding its due. Mead would probably say the United States bears some responsibility for the gap between the world's rich and poor, and, as the world's wealthiest country, could informally do far more to help those less advantaged. She would probably also lament the government's seeming unawareness of other cultures in formulating foreign policy.

Although Mead respected and embraced technology, she told the interviewer in 1958 that she did not anticipate major advances in the next fifty years (that is, by 2008) to be in technical inventions. Americans needed to learn what kind of help to give a third-world country "to knit itself into a new nationhood" and how "to work out communication between one group of people and another." What we need, she said, "are human sciences—to educate people how to live in this new world and how to develop social inventions that will make it possible for us to survive" (Brandon 1969: 171). Mead would probably encourage the United States to expend more effort both in providing help and devising communication techniques.

A SHARED SENSE OF RESPONSIBILITY FOR HUMANKIND

> If you look closely, you will see that almost anything that really matters to us, anything that embodies our deepest commitment to the way human life should be lived and cared for, depends on some form—more often, many forms—of volunteerism.
> —Mead and Métraux, *Aspects of the Present* (1980)

In the dedication to their 1985 book *Only Mothers Know: Patterns of Infant Feeding in Traditional Cultures*, a book supportive of breastfeeding in all cultures, Dana Raphael and Flora Davis wrote, "To Margaret Mead whose lifetime was spent urging all of us '. . . about the importance of feeling responsibility to people we don't know yet and

may never see.'" Mead's sense of responsibility extended to volunteer
efforts large and small, from the government's helping poorer countries
to individual efforts. In an article for *Redbook* in September, 1975, she
wrote, "We desperately need volunteers to get work done" (Mead and
Métraux 1980: 90). Mead felt that volunteerism had been debased and
commercialized and noted the need to reestablish respect between professionals and volunteers by full acknowledgment that the volunteer is
carrying out necessary work. She also suggested volunteers receive tax
and social security credit along with reimbursement of expenses since
"Americans never have believed wholeheartedly that virtue should be
its sole—as well as its own— reward" (Mead and Métraux 1980: 90).
Mead would see little reason today to change her views.

GENERATION GAP, REPRISE

> It is only with the direct participation of the young . . .
> that we can build a viable future.
> —Mead, *Culture and Commitment* (1970)

The generation gap between adults and young people to which Mead
first made reference in the 1960s was based on differences in values. The
divide today is based not on ideology but on technology. Nevertheless,
Mead's comments about a prefigurative culture, that is, one in which
change is so rapid that children teach adults, continue to resonate. Mead
was not alive to witness the proliferation of computers, both in the home
and in the workplace, or the egalitarian use of the Internet, but she did
write in *Culture and Commitment* that "suddenly, because all the peoples
of the world are part of one electronically based, intercommunicating
network, young people everywhere share a kind of experience that none
of the elders ever have had or will have" (1970a: 50).

The elders, however, are scrambling to have electronic experiences,
with adults clamoring to take courses that will help them stay abreast
of current technology, but as Mead predicted, many adults rely on
young people to help them learn computer skills, program their VCRs,
and take digital photos they can quickly transmit electronically around
the world. Mead believed a role exists for adults in a prefigurative

society to develop "ways of teaching and learning that will keep the future open. We must create new models for adults who can teach their children not what to learn, but how to learn and not what they should be committed to, but the value of commitment" (1970a: 72). Adults, especially grandparents, said Mead, can fulfill this role. Because the elders in American society have witnessed so much change, they "now become those who best know how to prepare their grandchildren for innovation and change" (Mead and Heyman 1965: 124). Mead used the model of her own family, whose grandmother had been her primary teacher and had been "experimental, curious and exploratory, avid for new ideas on how to open the minds of small children" (Mead and Métraux 1980: 144).

Mead, who also welcomed innovation and change, could not conceive of grandparents being stuck in the past and would encourage their acceptance of change and continued learning. "Grandparents need grandchildren to keep the changing world alive for them," Mead wrote. "And grandchildren need grandparents to help them know who they are and to give them a sense of human experience in a world they cannot know" (Mead and Métraux 1980: 145).

DIVERSITY

> Our attempts nationally to bring together children who differ from one another in color, religion, language and in ethnic, economic and social background are still clumsy and crude.
> —Mead and Métraux, *A Way of Seeing* (1961)

Because Mead had learned from other cultures, she saw diversity as a resource from which all people can learn. Mead believed learning comes from observing other groups and transferring that information to personal issues. The website celebrating the 100th anniversary of Mead's birthday reads in part: "Thus, she insisted that human diversity is a resource, not a handicap, that all human beings have the capacity to learn from and teach each other" (http://www.mead2001.org).

Mead would welcome both learning from and teaching each other in a more diverse America. In *Rethinking Psychological Anthropology*, Philip Bock wrote in 1999, "It would be wonderful to report that racism and other forms of prejudice have diminished as a result of anthropological research and publication, but no figures of the stature of Ruth Benedict or Margaret Mead have arisen thus far to carry the message of cultural diversity and tolerance to the public" (23). While spokespeople of prominence might speed the process, shifting demographics in the United States would seem to indicate diversity and multiculturalism will eventually prevail.

CULTURAL RELATIVISM

> Looking ahead, another question each woman must ask herself is: How do you feel about other women?
> —Mead and Métraux, *Aspects of the Present* (1980)

Respecting diversity can be a double-edged sword. The world of the twenty-first century is moving beyond the view that all cultural traditions merit total acceptance. Richard Warms describes this problem:

> Boas and his students, including Mead, worked in an America that was in many ways profoundly racist and isolationist. It was a land where only men of Northern European descent were considered really fully true Americans; all others were members of lesser races. It was also a land where ideas, customs, and goods were prized because of their "Americanness" and there was deep suspicion of anything foreign. Boas and his students were utterly opposed to this vision of America and American culture. Using the notion of cultural relativism, they championed the rights of minorities and immigrants. They did this partially by standing for the notion that all cultures were equally valid and all humans equally civilized. They loudly proclaimed that there was no one right way to organize a human society and that all humans had equal capacity to create cultures. They lampooned the notion that there was any such thing as a pure American culture. In doing this, anthropologists played a critical part in the development of modern America.

Today, almost everyone in America has come to agree with Boas. We no longer believe in the superiority of the Northern European male and we recognize that our culture is full of ideas, goods, cuisine, and customs from many different cultures. We may be very glad and proud to be American citizens, but we no longer look at those who are from other cultures as fundamentally our inferiors. The very success of cultural relativism has, however, created problems. (R. Warms, personal communication, March 30, 2002)

The problems Warms mentions have immense implications for international relations:

Boasians emphasized the notion that, since cultures were the products of their own histories, there was no way to compare them. This meant that there could be no set of universal moral laws that apply to all cultures. That does not sound too bad until you realize that any notion of human rights would have to be a moral law applying to all cultures. So, how can we have human rights in a Boasian world? As human beings it is our obligation not only to express outrage but to take action against things such as genocide or slavery. But how, in a culturally relative world, do we have the moral authority to do so? Modern anthropologists are left applauding cultural relativism as a research tool but oft times deploring it as a philosophy. (R. Warms, personal communication, March 30, 2002)

No country is immune from using traditional cultural practices as an excuse for violating human rights. At a 1998 speech in Iran on women's rights, Maryam Namazie pointed out that cultural relativism "legitimizes and maintains savagery" (http://www.hambastegi.org) and even countries that denounce the West use the Western concept of cultural relativism to subjugate women and ignore human rights. She noted that, while all human beings are worthy of respect, the beliefs of all do not merit respect. Namazie gave the example of an eighteen-year-old woman burnt to death in Germany in 1997 when she refused to marry her father's choice for her husband. The court gave the father a reduced sentence because such murder was deemed acceptable in his culture and religion.

Other equally contentious examples include female circumcision, child labor, child marriages, acceptance of subhuman prison conditions in less advanced countries, religious persecution, and forced veiling of women. Broad and bitter differences exist about traditions that are culturally acceptable and those that are intolerable transgressions of human rights.

Such issues influence personal decision making. When traveling, should an American female wear shorts in a country in which bare legs are considered offensive, even when the temperature is ninety degrees? Personal choices require consideration of the host country, since acceptable behavior in the United States may be seen as unconventional elsewhere. At home, one must decide to what extent to investigate, honor, and respect the traditions and values of another culture.

What would Mead say? Dr. Warms suspects that her commitment to the Episcopal Church was her answer to not accepting a pure form of cultural relativism, as was Boas's commitment to the Society for Ethical Humanism.

BIRTHING

> Birth itself is strongly patterned everywhere. . . . The mother's position during child-birth is determined by the culture. She may squat or kneel or bear down on a rope suspended from the roof, or she may be supported by her husband or female relatives, or friends.
> —Mead, *Cultural Patterns and Technical Change* (1955)

Mead was supportive of a culture's birthing practices, but also believed in the use of scientific knowledge that protects the health of mothers and newborns. Dana Raphael says:

> If Margaret Mead were alive today I believe she would think that she should tell young women not to believe that childbirth is any more a normal or natural event. With epidurals and monitors and episiotomies and drips and antibiotics etc. etc., it certainly is no longer— natural. I would think she would tell of the many births she witnessed in the field where the mother who had most recently delivered was expected to attend the birthing woman. She would tell of the disposal

of the placenta and the umbilical cord under the steps of the entrance way in some places in the globe and suggest newly delivered women and their partners might wish to save the cord and the placenta. She would remind them that during the 1930s there was a group in the US called the placental eaters. She would ask the future mother to go on the web and check out all her options and all the consequences of each. She would say the same about the statistical aspects of the birthing center or the hospital she has chosen. That is, she would suggest they check to see where, when and to whom the C-sections were performed and compare the number of epidermals in each birthing center. She would expect the partner to help but have enough sense to step aside if a woman-to-woman interaction was appropriate.

She would order us to be sensitive to the women who have abortions or whose fetus dies in utero or at birth.

She would tell them to keep notes on the child's development because we are asking today's kids to break every former record and she would wonder what is being done to children to make that possible. (D. Raphael, personal communication, March 23, 2002)

CHILDREN AND FAMILIES

> At least two adults are needed in a home with growing children.
> —Mead and Métraux, *Aspects of the Present* (1980)

Mead recognized that many family situations, like the one in which she was reared and in which she reared her daughter, are not composed of the cookie-cutter mother, father, and two children. She acknowledged the possibility of many configurations of adults but recommended children have at least two adults who share a "continuing, loving and responsible relationship with each other and with the children living there" (Mead and Métraux 1980: 138). In her usual way of uniquely interpreting a situation, she noted that a single adult tends to monotonously maintain discussions at the child's level and the adult has no one with whom to share household tasks and conversation, but when a second adult is present, the child tends to be challenged by conversation and the adults provide support to each other.

Mead also believed that too much research and study have focused on why children do not grow into successful adults instead of the more positive ways in which their environment makes them strong. She described how a doctor rescued two small children, sick emotionally and physically from life in a Nazi concentration camp, after World War II. He nurtured them and they grew and prospered. The doctor, curious as to how they had the strength not only to survive but also to grow to lead a meaningful life, traced their early years. He found their grandmother, who told him about their mother's support and love when they were tiny. "From medicine and psychology, we have learned how badly damaged children can be. Not enough emphasis has been put on the ways in which children can also be made especially strong" (Mead 1968: 29).

EDUCATION

> You know what college material is—something you put into a college like meat into a sausage machine.
> —Mead, "Uniqueness and Universality" (1974)

Mead told an interviewer that American parents expect children to do well in school, handle any situation well, and be successful "whereas in some other countries they bring docility, obedience, respect. In every culture of the world children bring something to their parents—and the parents give them love, reward, punishment, in return" (Brandon 1969: 167).

Although Mead had limited formal education herself prior to high school, she quickly became a well-known authority on educational issues. She concerned herself with every aspect of education, from nursery school to college, from the child's bus ride to school through his or her instructional program, from gifted students to those with special needs.

In 1927, before *Coming of Age in Samoa* stirred public imagination, Mead's article "The Need for Teaching Anthropology in Normal Schools and Teachers' Colleges" was published in School and Society. She emphasized the attributes of anthropology as a discipline that enabled people to objectively study and analyze other cultures in a way that allowed generalization to their own.

Mead soon began to develop a thread visible in her views about education, first on the ability of schools to transmit culture, later on their ability not only to convey but also to change a culture. In a 1931 article for *Progressive Education* she was already taking positions that countered current trends, foreshadowing her inclination to surprise and shock, when she argued that schools should pass along a cultural inheritance to the children and not allow children's creativity to determine what takes place in the classroom, with the result that something entirely new is produced. This viewpoint was probably not typical of most of the journal's readers.

By 1943, Mead recognized the ability of education to convey one's culture and to change it. She saw the trend for children to educationally move beyond that of their parents and observed that a feeling of superiority was pushing one group's culture to become the norm, to the detriment of diversity. "It is in this article that Mead takes a strong position toward education as a transformative tool in culture change—a position which will be expanded throughout her next 30 years of writing and research—but a position from which she will not back down" (Monroe 1992: 13).

By 1950, Mead was adamant that the atomic age had changed the educational scene and that a teacher had to perform multiple functions, including educating youth to live in a rapidly changing world. By the 1960s, she envisioned education and work as intermittently occurring throughout one's life, with youth needing to work and adults needing to study.

Mead's writings on education during the 1970s drew on her insights about other cultures and she believed social unrest throughout the world was caused by obsolete educational systems. In the United States Mead advised adults in positions of authority to learn from younger teachers and students. She considered a good teacher to be one who does not make assumptions but takes the trouble to find out what students know and who is persistent in trying new ways of repeating instruction for the child who has difficulties learning. "In a sense," she wrote, "good teachers always suffer fools gladly" (Mead 1979: 196).

Mead called children the country's youngest "commuters." If parents disliked a long commute to and from work, the trip was equally onerous for children, and Mead declared that busing youngsters great distances was a poor way to solve social problems like school integration (Mead and Métraux 1980: 177). She also suggested that time spent on school buses could be used to memorize, since memory training was neglected in the schools. Obviously, students did not enthusiastically accept this idea.

"Sociocultural approaches to learning and development," wrote Diane Torres-Velasquez, "are based on the concept that human activities are situated in cultural contexts, are mediated by language and other symbolic systems of representation, and are best understood in their historical context" (2000: 3). "The City as the Portal of the Future," written with her sister Elizabeth Steig, illustrated a wide-reaching sociocultural approach as well as points Mead frequently emphasized. The article provided practical and useful ideas and included a vision of cities as the hope for future world peace. It was written in everyday language, with optimism permeating the entire article. Like many of Mead's articles, it focused a great deal on early childhood education, as she believed the very young were more receptive; "we realize very acutely that this is the age we have a chance" (Mead 1974b: 60).

In the article, based on Mead's study of human settlements, Mead and Steig envisioned a future world of city-states in which people freely moved. The city in the changed world of 1964, Mead and Steig wrote, was responsible for "rearing children and preparing adults for a world almost, but not quite, here" (148). They suggested that cities can provide a laboratory for children to learn safely about the world, just as the countryside once was the place where children developed a practical approach to life.

Cities, they wrote, can teach spatial relationships. Children will learn about their neighborhoods by drawing and building replicas and dioramas of them. By standing at the top of a tall building or a mountain and looking down at the tiny people below, they can experience and gain an understanding of far space. "Every group of children who stand with bated breath looking up at a high ceiling or down from a high balcony or who dash down a long empty avenue on a Sunday morning after a fall of snow will take back to their classrooms something which will be reflected in their drawing, their modeling, their sculpture, their understanding of their school books" (150).

But, the article continued, children need bounded space that provides a sense of security and warmth, such as alcoves and schoolrooms in which they learn to organize their environment. Different parts of the schoolroom can reflect different time zones and "relative times and distances can be paced out in human steps, calibrated to thousands of miles" (150).

Children should also transform their neighborhoods by cleaning up playgrounds and planting flowers in gardens or containers. They can learn about accepting limits and the need for an orderly world by comparison with other neighborhoods. Finally, children should be presented with varied experiences in a three-dimensional natural and constructed world throughout their schooling, not just in the early years. Mead and Steig did not see a single teacher as carrying out the task they envisioned but suggested that older children and adults volunteer their help. The article, in reconfiguring the city as an entrance to the future, provided practical ideas for individual teachers, but it also suggested impossibly idealistic and impractical solutions.

Mead was never one to shrink from utopian ideas. As with positions on other societal concerns, her innovative solutions to American educational problems were lofty and comprehensive. Administrators should periodically return to the classroom, she wrote. She also recognized the value of writing being considered a process rather than simply a product long before the schools emphasized the importance of students as authors.

Mead was especially concerned about excessive pressure put on young adults to continue their education, "which turns many schools into places where young people respond either as prisoners, or as the irresponsible members of a drafted peacetime army whiling the time away" (Mead 1961b: 39). Mead's 1961 description of a holding program sounds eerily similar to those in a 2001 book for school leaders. *Educating All Students Together* notes the significant numbers of students, beyond those enrolled in special education, for whom "school is not about success in learning. For these students, school is somewhere they go because they have to. School does not foster their learning, nor does it challenge them to become independent workers or active citizens. School is where they go until they can go somewhere else to do that which is important to them" (Burrello, Lashley, and Beatty 2001: 1). Even with her bent for optimism, Mead would have to admit lack of results in finding solutions to the problem of disaffected young adults being maintained within a school setting.

The success of the G.I. Bill, which funded college for those who served during World War II, prompted Mead's idea to help mature students who later see the value of an education. Mead suggested that students who performed two years of service either nationally or internationally should receive vouchers to continue their education, an education for which they might then be receptive. She thought that young people needed "a period when youth can find itself. Instead we have a society organized to push each individual directly from childhood into adulthood" (Mead 1961b: 46).

Mead's thinking was also progressive in other areas relative to educating children. In the early years of the twentieth century, intelligence was seen as a static number that could be obtained by administering a test, the result for which was linked to heredity. Mead recognized that such tests were biased against those for whom English was not their primary language; thus, many immigrants were assumed to have low intelligence. Building on her mother's research, Mead's master's thesis recognized that a person's primary language, socioeconomic status, and length of time in the United States impacted performance on an intelligence test. This concept seems logical and obvious, but it was considered radical in the 1920s.

When the words *mainstreaming* and *inclusion* became part of the language of special education in the 1970s, Mead had been advocating for many years the education of students as whole persons included in all facets of society. This was an insight Mead first presented in *Coming of Age in Samoa*. In chapter 11, "The Girl in Conflict," and in appendix 4, "The Mentally Defective and the Mentally Diseased," Mead described the few cases of individuals with disabilities she noted. Although her language included terminology prevalent in the field of psychology in the 1920s, she reflected on Samoan charity toward people with weaknesses. In 1959 she gave the example of a young woman with Down's syndrome who was accepted by a religious community and who, by her inclusion into a broadened lifestyle, became a whole person (Smith 1998: 197).

Educating children with special needs is, however, a costly business and with twenty-first-century science allowing the birth and survival of babies who not long ago would have perished, immense human and technological resources are required to assist with their education. Given that, as Rayna Rapp noted in her April 2001 Barnard conference presentation, "the study of complex genetic traits intersect the exquisitely stratified world of special education," the education of students with special needs is primed to meet head-on with science. What would Mead say?

THE ROLE OF SCIENCE

> **The answer is not to limit research. What is needed instead is careful and profound discussion based on the best knowledge we have—knowledge that is shared and understood by all responsible citizens, not only those who are scientists.**
> **—Mead, *Margaret Mead: Some Personal Views* (1979)**

Mead once quipped that fathers were biologically but not socially necessary. As technology leads to alternative ways to create new life, this idea becomes less true. Scientific knowledge is no longer an isolated concept. It is becoming a social force, with culture, emerging genetic technologies, medicine, and ethics coming together.

Rapp pointed out that "the subject of reproduction and its scientific control sits on the rhetorical divide between nature and culture, connecting the past and the future not only of individuals and social groups, but of nations, as well" (2001). The ramifications, Mead would say, require dialogue among disciplines, with the inclusion of private citizens. Rapp concluded that Mead would have "used the famous thumb-stick, pointing our attention to the intersection of reproductive technologies and disability consciousness, saying, 'Now watch this very carefully.'"

A FINAL WORD

> Never doubt that a small group of thoughtful, committed citizens can change the world.
>
> —Mead, http://www.mead2001.org

Mead fervently believed that a few committed people could provoke change, and the above remark is her most cited quotation. Many concerns she raised might not be twenty-first-century problems if people had joined together at that time to insist corrective action be taken. Although she was known to voice the idea frequently and in slightly varied ways, when and where Mead initially said those exact words is unknown, but the quote has been used by many organizations working for societal change, often with the additional words, "In fact, it's the only thing that ever has" (http://www.mead2001.org).

Mead herself did not change the world, but she changed the way Americans think about the world. She reached so high and so wide in her ideas that her influence on the way people in the twenty-first century think is still both pervasive and substantial. Margaret Mead pushed Americans to reflect on themselves and on other cultures. And she did it with flair and panache.

NOTES

CHAPTER 1

1. The two states outside the continental United States, Hawaii and Alaska, both gained statehood in 1959.

2. In the early 1900s many parents viewed work as a valid reason to keep children out of school, if the children were needed for farm labor, household chores, and care of younger children. Children also worked in factories and even coal mines, since it was not until 1938 that the Fair Labor Standards Act, nationally prohibiting child labor under age sixteen (age eighteen for hazardous jobs), was passed.

CHAPTER 2

1. Using documents obtained from the FBI under the Freedom of Information Act, David Price traced the validity of Boas's charge in a November 20, 2000, issue of the *Nation*, and urged the AAA to examine the implications of their continuing refusal to denounce the use of social science as a cover for covert activities. See chapter 7.

CHAPTER 3

1. Ironically, the comment of her father, an avowed agnostic, derives from Jesus's remark to a man who sought to follow him: "No one who puts his hand to the plow and looks back is fit for the kingdom of God." The verse cautions those who walk behind a plow not to look back lest they waver and plow an uneven row and, by extension, not to waver in their religious beliefs. The verse may date from earlier usage but is recorded in Luke 9:62. Thanks to the Reverend Columba Gilliss, Grace Episcopal Church, New Market, Maryland, for her insights.

CHAPTER 5

1. The sacred flute presented to Mead and Fortune is now on display in the Hall of Pacific Peoples at the American Museum of Natural History, catalogue number 80.0/8437 AB.

2. The Mundugumor kinship system was exceptionally complicated, and McDowell found an incorrect interpretation Mead herself made.

3. This is the model Mary Catherine Bateson, the daughter of Margaret and Gregory, presented in her memoirs, *With a Daughter's Eye* (1984: 166). She also noted (302) that Mead reversed east and west on page 238 of *Blackberry Winter*.

4. It remained for Isabel Briggs Myers and Katherine Myers with the *Myers-Briggs Type Indicator* (MBTI) and David Keirsey with *Portraits of Temperament* to refine and redefine individual temperament theory. See Berens 1998, and Wirths and Bowman-Kruhm 1992.

5. Culture and personality is considered by some as a school of thought within psychological anthropology rather than synonymous with it.

6. Mead reports staying six months in New Guinea (1972: 261). Jacknis reports a stay of eight months, with return to Bali in February 1939 (1988: 162).

CHAPTER 6

1. Mary M. Wolfskill, Head, Reference and Reader Service Section, Manuscript Division, Library of Congress, wrote that these papers are located in folder 17, container I 28 (M. M. Wolfskill, personal communication, February 13, 2002).

2. Conflicting dates are reported about whether she was home two or five days. Mead reported the latter in Benedict's *American Anthropologist* obituary.

3. After Ted and Lenora Schwartz divorced, Lenora remarried and is later referred to by the name Lenora Foerstel.

4. Papua New Guinea gained independence in 1975.

5. For an extensive discussion of somatotyping, including Roll's follow-up studies of the Pere villagers and her friendship with Margaret Mead, refer to Barbara Honeyman Heath Roll's transcribed oral history at http://sunsite .berkeley.edu:2020/dynaweb/teiproj/oh/science.

CHAPTER 7

1. One exception were the notes on the Mundugumor taken by Mead and Fortune on their second trip to New Guinea. Although Mead used her material in *Sex and Temperament in Three Primitive Societies* and other writings for the popular press, many notes remained unpublished. Fortune eventually transferred his notes to Mead, who began the task of organizing them. Nancy McDowell continued Mead's work after her death and subsequently turned them into the book The Mundugumor. See chapter 5.

2. This term is attributed to Peter Worsley in *Confronting the Margaret Mead Legacy,* but Foerstel and Gilliam note that Worsley informed them that he "first heard this phrase from British anthropologist E. E. Evans-Pritchard" (1992: 146).

3. Mead was not Dr. Salovesh's source for information about her rescue contribution to the AAA and he does not feel free to tell how he knows about it, but says he has independent confirmation from three sources and believes the story is accurate. As far as he knows, Mead never mentioned her AAA contributions in public.

4. Also spelled "de Barraza."

CHAPTER 8

1. *Hamlet,* act I, scene II, line 188: "I shall not look upon his like again."

2. In her oral history, Barbara Honeyman Heath Roll said Mead worked on *Blackberry Winter* while on her 1968 trip to Pere village.

3. In *Coming of Age in Samoa*, Mead mentions both "nine months" (10) and "six months" (260).

4. Mead is imprecise with her data for the total number of villagers and the total number of subjects studied. Given the small number of subjects Mead studied and the census she took but did not publish of the villages where she collected data, one would expect numbers to be concise and consistent. Instead, Mead rounds off the number in the locale studied at 600. The unpublished census, according to Martin Orans, yields a population of 785, although counting the numbers in two of the three villages gives a population of 555; the girls studied, however, also came from a third village.

Similarly, no matter how the number of girls interviewed is counted, the numbers do not tally. Mead wrote that she observed 68 girls (260). Adding the numbers she next provides—28 with no sign of puberty, 14 who would mature within next year, and 25 who passed puberty within the last four years (261)—gives a total of 67. Counting the number in each category in the schematic of villages (251–253) gives a total of 72.

Mead differentiated between number of girls "studied" and number of girls "studied in detail," but again these numbers are not consistent. She wrote that she "studied in detail" 50 girls (11 and app. 5), but includes a categorization of 28 prepubescent girls, 14 near puberty, and 25 who had passed puberty, for a total of 67 (app. 2).

GLOSSARY

animism. Belief that animals, objects, and natural phenomena have spirits and souls.

anthropology. An interdisciplinary science that looks at ancient and modern peoples; the four main branches are social or cultural anthropology, biological or physical anthropology, linguistics, and archaeology.

applied anthropology. Anthropology used to solve a practical problem, such as recognizing cultural preferences when distributing food after a disaster.

cultural relativism. The belief that all cultures have value and that no culture is superior to another; by extension, the shared attitudes, values, morals, goals, and patterns of behavior of a culture should be accepted by other cultures.

ethnography. Observation, recordation, and analysis of data obtained when studying the customs and social organization of a society.

event analysis. Observing and systematically recording detailed information about an event.

lavalava. Wide loincloth made of cotton and twisted to fasten the material at the waist; worn by both men and women.

matai. Samoan titled person, such as a chief or talking chief; head of a large household.

Melanesia. Pacific islands that lie northeast of Australia and south of Micronesia; included are the Bismarck Archipelago, Solomon, Vanuatu, New Caledonia, and Fiji groups.

Micronesia. Pacific islands that lie east of the Philippines and north of Melanesia; included are the Caroline, Mariana, and Marshall groups.

Oceania. General geographic term for the islands of the central and south Pacific; included are Micronesia, Melanesia, Polynesia (including New Zealand), and Australia. The Malay Archipelago is sometimes included.

participant observation. Immersing oneself in all possible aspects of the culture one is studying.

primitive society. In anthropology, generally a preliterate society (i.e., without a written language of its own). Other names often used include *precontact* and *traditional.*

psychological anthropology. Research into culture and personality that includes the fields of cultural and social anthropology and the psychology of personality.

sago. Powdered or granulated starch prepared from the sago palm and used in cooking.

schismogenesis. Progressive evolutionary changes in relationships among either individuals or groups.

tapa. Coarse cloth made from tree bark that is pounded and then decorated with geometric designs.

Tok Pisin. Previously called *pidgin English*, a language combining various native tongues coupled with words derived from English. Also called *Neo-Melanesian*.

BIBLIOGRAPHY

Works by Margaret Mead

1927. "The Need for Teaching Anthropology in Normal Schools and Teachers' Colleges." *School and Society,* 26, 8 October, 466–468.

1928. "The Role of the Individual in Samoan Culture." *Journal of the Royal Anthropological Institute of Great Britain and Ireland,* 58, 481–495.

1931. "The Meaning of Freedom in Education." *Progressive Education,* 8, February, 107–111.

1937. ed. *Cooperation and Competition Among Primitive Peoples.* New York: McGraw-Hill.

1942. *And Keep Your Powder Dry: An Anthropologist Looks at America.* New York: William Morrow.

1949a. *Male and Female: A Study of the Sexes in a Changing World.* New York: William Morrow.

1949b. "Ruth Fulton Benedict, 1887–1948." *American Anthropologist,* 51, 457–463.

1951a. "The Impact of Culture on Personality Development in the US Today." *Understanding the Child,* 20, 17–18.

1951b. *Soviet Attitudes Toward Authority: An Interdisciplinary Approach to Problems of Soviet Character.* New York: The RAND Corporation/ McGraw-Hill.

1956. *New Lives for Old: Cultural Transformation—Manus, 1928–1953.* New York: William Morrow.

1961a. *Coming of Age in Samoa: A Psychological Study of Primitive Youth for Western Civilization.* New York: Morrow Quill Paperbacks. (Original work published 1928.)

1961b. ed. "The Young Adult." In E. Ginzberg, *Values and Ideals of American Youth* (37–51). New York: Columbia University Press.

1962. *Growing Up in New Guinea: A Comparative Study of Primitive Education.* New York: William Morrow. (Original work published 1930.)

1963a. ed. *Cultural Patterns and Technical Change.* New York: New American Library. (Original work published 1955.)

1963b. *Sex and Temperament in Three Primitive Societies.* New York: William Morrow. (Original work published 1935.)

1965a. *Anthropologists and What They Do*. New York: Franklin Watts. (Original work published 1959.)

1965b. "The Future as the Basis for Establishing a Shared Culture." *Daedalus*, 94, Winter, 135–153.

1967. *The Changing Cultural Patterns of Work and Leisure*. Washington, DC: US Department of Labor.

1968. *A Creative Life for Your Children*. Washington, DC: US Department of Health, Education, and Welfare, Social and Rehabilitation Service, Children's Bureau. (Original work published 1962.)

1970a. *Culture and Commitment: A Study of the Generation Gap*. Garden City, NY: Natural History Press/Doubleday.

1970b. *Hunger*. New York: Scientists' Institute for Public Information.

1972. *Blackberry Winter: My Earlier Years*. New York: Pocket Books.

1973a. ed. *An Anthropologist at Work: Writings of Ruth Benedict*. New York: Equinox Books. (Original work published 1959.)

1973b. "Changing Styles of Anthropological Work." *Annual Review of Anthropology*, 2, 1–26.

1973c. "Rights to Life." *Christianity and Crisis*, 8 January, 288–292.

1974a. *Ruth Benedict*. New York: Columbia University Press.

1974b. "Uniqueness and Universality." *Childhood Education*, 51, November-December, 58–63.

1977. *Letters from the Feld, 1925–1975*. New York: Harper & Row.

1979. *Margaret Mead: Some Personal Views*. (R. Métraux, Ed.). New York: Walker.

Mead, M., and P. Byers. 1968. *The Small Conference: An Innovation in Communication*. Paris: Mouton.

Mead, M., and K. Heyman. 1965. *Family*. New York: Macmillan.

———. 1975. *World Enough: Rethinking the Future*. Boston: Little, Brown.

Mead, M., and R. Métraux, eds. 1953. *The Study of Culture at a Distance*. Chicago: University of Chicago Press.

———. 1970. *A Way of Seeing*. New York: McCall. (Original work published 1961.)

———. 1980. *Aspects of the Present*. New York: William Morrow.

Mead, M., and E. Steig. 1964. "The City as the Portal of the Future." *Journal of Nursery Education*, 19, April, 146–153.

BOOKS AND CHAPTERS

Allen, F. L. 1940. *Since Yesterday.* New York: Harper & Brothers.

———. 1952. *The Big Change.* New York: Harper & Brothers.

Barnouw, V. 1979. *Culture and Personality.* ed. 3rd. Homewood, IL: Dorsey Press.

Bateson, M. C. 1984. *With a Daughter's Eye: A Memoir of Margaret Mead and Gregory Bateson.* New York: Pocket Books.

Bateson, M. C., R. Birdwhistell,, J. Brockman, D. Lipset, R. May, M. Mead, et al. 1977. *About Bateson.* ed. J. Brockman. New York: E. P. Dutton.

Berens, L. 1998. *Understanding Yourself and Others: An Introduction to Temperaments.* Huntington Beach, CA: Telos Publications.

Bock, P. K. 1999. *Rethinking Psychological Anthropology: Continuity and Change in the Study of Human Action,* 2nd ed. Prospect Heights, IL: Waveland Press.

Brandon, H. 1969. "A Conversation with Margaret Mead." In J. C. Mickelson, ed., *American Personality and the Creative Arts,* 163–171. Minneapolis, MN: Burgess.

Brockman, J. 1977. "Introduction." In J. Brockman, ed., *About Bateson,* 3–20. New York: E. P. Dutton.

Brogan, D. W. "The American Personality: A Critique of New World Culture." In J. C. Mickelson, ed., *American Personality and the Creative Arts,* 51–62. Minneapolis, MN: Burgess.

Burne, J. 1989. *Chronicle of the World.* New York: Ecam.

Burrello, L. C., C. Lashley, and E. E. Beatty. 2001. *Educating All Students Together: How School Leaders Create Unified Systems.* Thousand Oaks, CA: Corwin.

Campbell, J., ed. 1986. *The Portable Jung.* New York: Penguin.

Cassidy, R. 1982. *Margaret Mead: A Voice for the Century.* New York: Universe Books.

Cressman, L. S. 1988. *A Golden Journey: Memoirs of an Archaeologist.* Salt Lake City: University of Utah Press.

Epstein, S., and B. Epstein. 1980. *She Never Looked Back: Margaret Mead in Samoa.* New York: Coward, McCann & Geoghegan.

Foerstel, L., and A. Gilliam, eds. 1992. *Confronting the Margaret Mead Legacy: Scholarship, Empire, and the South Pacific.* Philadelphia: Temple University Press.

Freeman, D. 1983. *Margaret Mead and Samoa: The Making and Unmaking of an Anthropological Myth.* Cambridge: Harvard University Press.

————.1999. *The Fateful Hoaxing of Margaret Mead.* Boulder, CO: Westview Press.

Glidewell, J. C. 1970. *Choice Points: Essays on the Emotional Problems of Living with People.* Cambridge: Massachusetts Institute of Technology Press.

Grinager, P. 1999. *Uncommon Lives: My Lifelong Friendship with Margaret Mead.* Lanham, MD: Rowman & Littlefield.

Grosskurth, P. 1988. *Margaret Mead.* New York: Penguin Books.

Howard, J. 1984. *Margaret Mead: A Life.* New York: Fawcett Columbine.

Lapsley, H. 1999. *Margaret Mead and Ruth Benedict: The Kinship of Women.* Amherst: University of Massachusetts Press.

Lipset, D. 1977. "Gregory Bateson: Early Biography." In J. Brockman, ed., *About Bateson*, 21–54. New York: E. P. Dutton.

MacClancy, J., and C. McDonaugh, eds. 1996. *Popularizing Anthropology.* New York: Routledge.

Mainzer, R., L. Mainzer, B. Lowry, P. Baltzley, and J. Nunn. 1996. *The Cooperative Collaborative Process: The Fundamentals.* Baltimore: Johns Hopkins University Press.

McDowell, N. 1991. *The Mundugumor: From the Feld Notes of Margaret Mead and Reo Fortune.* Washington, DC: Smithsonian Institution Press.

McGee, R. J., and R. L. Warms. 1996. *Anthropological Theory: An Introductory History.* Mountain View, CA: Mayfield.

Mickelson, J. C., ed. 1969. *American Personality and the Creative Arts.* Minneapolis, MN: Burgess.

Mitchell, W. E. 1996. "Communicating Culture." In J. MacClancy and C. McDonaugh, eds., *Popularizing Anthropology*, 122–134. New York: Routledge.

Monroe, S. S. 1992. *Margaret Mead: Anthropological Perspective on Educational Change.* Washington, DC: Office of Educational Research and Improvement. (ERIC Document Reproduction Service no. ED356168.)

Murphey, M. 1969. "Culture, Character, and Personality." In J. C. Mickelson, ed., *American Personality and the Creative Arts*, 37–50. Minneapolis, MN: Burgess.

Orans, M. 1996. *Not Even Wrong: Margaret Mead, Derek Freeman, and the Samoans.* Novato, CA: Chandler and Sharp.

Pycior, H. M., N. G. Slack, and P. G. Abir-Am, eds. 1996. *Creative Couples in the Sciences.* New Brunswick, NJ: Rutgers University Press.

Raphael, D. 1973. *The Tender Gift: Breastfeeding.* New York: Schocken Books.

Raphael, D., and F. Davis. 1985. *Only Mothers Know: Patterns of Infant Feeding in Traditional Cultures.* Westport, CT: Greenwood.

Sapir, E. 1927. "The Unconscious Patterning of Behavior in Society." In E. S. Dummer, ed. *The Unconscious: A Symposium.* New York: Alfred A. Knopf.

Sullivan, G. 1999. *Margaret Mead, Gregory Bateson, and Highland Bali: Fieldwork Photographs of Bayung Gedé, 1936–1939.* Chicago: University of Chicago Press.

Sykes, R. E. 1969. "The Culture Concept as Keystone." In J. C. Mickelson, ed., *American Personality and the Creative Arts,* 28–36. Minneapolis, MN: Burgess.

Von Hoffman, N., and G. B. Trudeau. 1979. *Tales from the Margaret Mead Taproom.* Kansas City: Andrews and McMeel.

Wakin, E. 1992. *Anthropology Goes to War: Professional Ethics and Counterinsurgency in Thailand.* Madison, WI: Center for Southeast Asia Studies.

Warner, C. 1992. *Treasury of Women's Quotations.* Englewood Cliffs, NJ: Prentice-Hall.

Wirths, C., and M. Bowman-Kruhm. 1992. *Are You My Type? Or Why Aren't You More Like Me?* Palo Alto, CA: Consulting Psychologists Press.

ARTICLES, SPEECHES, AND LETTERS

Carroll, T. G. 1990. "Who Owns Culture?" *Education and Urban Society,* 22, August, 346–355.

de Brigard, E. 1983. "Review of: Margaret Mead: Taking Note." *American Anthropologist,* 85, 494–495.

Du Bois, C. 1954. "Review of: *The Study of Culture at a Distance.*" *The Annals of the American Academy of Political and Social Sciences,* March, 176–177.

Eggan, F. 1974. "Among the Anthropologists." *Annual Review of Anthropology,* 3, 1–19.

Fraser, D. 1955. "Mundugamor Sculpture: Comments on the Art of a New Guinea Tribe." *Man,* 55, 17–20.

Hunter, E. 1989. "Educators Quest to Confront the World of the Twenty-first Century. *NASSP Bulletin,* 73, February, 1–7.

Jacknis, I. 1988. "Margaret Mead and Gregory Bateson in Bali: Their Use of Photography and Film." *Cultural Anthropology,* 3, 160–177.

Lee, J. A. 1999. "Why Our Children Have Rejected Traditional Values." Electronic version. *St. Croix Review,* December, 29–32.

Leonardo, M. Di. 2001. "Margaret Mead vs. Tony Soprano." Electronic version. *Nation,* 272, 21 May, 20:29, 6.

Library of Congress. (a). Margaret Mead: Letter to Martha Ramsey Mead, 11 March, 1923. Typescript. Manuscript Division (38).

Library of Congress. (b). Margaret Mead: Letter to Ruth Benedict, 11 October, 1925. Holograph manuscript. Manuscript Division (52).

Library of Congress. (c). Letter to Robert Lowie, 8 April, 1956. Typescript carbon. Manuscript Division (291a).

MacDougall, D. 1978. "Ethnographic Film: Failure and Promise." *Annual Review of Anthropology,* 7, 405–425.

"Margaret Mead Today: Mother to the World." 1969. *Time,* 74, 21 March.

Neumann, K. 1995. "Review of: Confronting the Margaret Mead Legacy: Scholarship, Empire, and the South Pacific." Electronic version. *Oceania,* 66, December, 161–162.

Newman, L. M. 1996. "Coming of Age, but Not in Samoa: Reflections on Margaret Mead's Legacy for Western Liberal Feminism." Electronic version. *American Quarterly,* 48(2), 233–272.

Pratt, F. 1981. "Teaching and Learning about Change." *Intercom,* 99, 31–32.

Price, D. 2000. "Anthropologists as Spies." Electronic version. *Nation,* 271, 20 Novmber, 26:24, 4.

Rapp, R. 2001. *Reconfiguring Human Nature.* Unpublished paper presented at the Margaret Mead Centennial, New York City, 6 April.

Sargeant, W. 1961. "It's All Anthropology." *New Yorker,* 30 December, 31–44.

Scheper-Hughes, N. 1984. "The Margaret Mead Controversy: Culture, Biology and Anthropological Inquiry." *Human Organization,* 43, 85–93.

Shinn, R. L. 1978. "I Miss You, Margaret." *Christianity and Crisis,* 11 December, 304–306.

Smith, J. D. 1998. "Histories of Special Education: Stories from Our Past, Insights for Our Future." *Remedial and Special Education,* 19, July–August, 196–200.

Smith, J. D., and G. L. Johnson, Jr. 1997. "Margaret Mead and Mental Retardation: Words of Understanding, Concepts of Inclusiveness." *Mental Retardation,* 35, August, 306–309.

Stewart, C. 1992. "The Popularization of Anthropology." *Anthropology Today,* 8(4), August, 15–16.

Stocking, G. 1992. "From Spencer to E-P: Eyewitnessing the Progress of Feldwork." *American Anthropologist,* 94, 398–400.

Torres-Velasquez, D. 2000. "Sociocultural Theory: Standing at the Cross-roads." Electronic version. *Remedial and Special Education,* 21, March-April, 2:66, 4.

Whitman, A. 1978. "Margaret Mead Is Dead of Cancer at 76." March-April, *New York Times,* A1, D18.

Worth, S. 1980. "Margaret Mead and the Shift from 'Visual Anthropology' to the 'Anthropology of Visual Communication.'" *Studies in Visual Communication,* 6(1), 15–22.

ELECTRONIC MEDIA

http://kenheyman.com. Website of Ken Heyman, photographer and collaborator with Mead.

http://sunsite.berkeley.edu:2020/dynaweb/teiproj/oh/science. Website maintained by the University of California–Berkeley Library, Regional Oral History Office. Includes "A Woman's Life in Physical Anthropology, Samototyping, and New Guinea Kinship Studies," interviews conducted from 1989 to 1991 by Sally Smith Hughes with Barbara Honeyman Heath Roll.

http://www.mead2001.org. Website to commemorate the 100th anniversary of Margaret Mead's birth.

Harley, B. 2001. "Education Abroad—Going Native or Standing Firm: Cultural Relativism." *Transitions Abroad.* January-February. From http://www.transabroad.com/publications/magazine/0101/activist.shtml. (accessed October 18, 2001).

Library of Congress. (d). "Margaret Mead: Excerpts from the First Diary of Margaret Mead, Begun on May 14, 1911." From http://lcweb.loc.gov/loc/kidslc/klmm.html. (accessed April 3, 2002).

Library of Congress. (e). "Margaret Mead: Letter to Martha Ramsay Mead, December 7, 1923." American Memory: Historical Collections of the National Digital Library. Manuscript Division—Selected Highlights. Women's History. From http://memory.loc.gov/mss/mcc/037/0001.jpg. (accessed July 16, 2001).

Namazie, M. 1998. *Cultural Relativism: This Era's Fascism.* From http://www.hambastegi.org. (accessed October 18, 2001).

AUDIOVISUAL MEDIA

Terkel, S. (Interviewer, WFMT/Chicago). 1993. *Four Decades with Studs Terkel*. (Cassette Recording no. 1–56511–003-X). St. Paul, MN: High-Bridge Co.

INDEX

Note: MM = Margaret Mead

ABOUT THE AUTHOR

MARY BOWMAN-KRUHM is the author of more than thirty books for children and young adults, including *The Leakeys: A Biography*, which is also available from Prometheus Books. She is a faculty associate at Johns Hopkins University's School of Education, Center for Technology in Eduation. More on the author can be found at www.marybk.com.

DATE DUE

BRODART, CO. Cat. No. 23-221